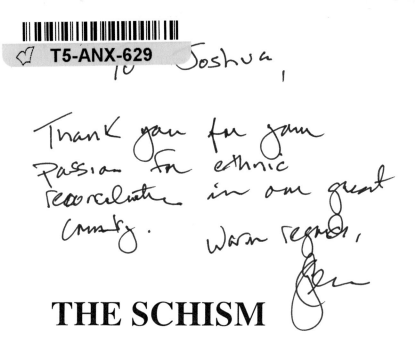

To Joshua,

Thank you for your passion for ethnic reconciliation in our great country.

Warm regards,

THE SCHISM

The Great Failure
of the American Evangelical Church

Glenn B. Davis

PRESS

To my treasured friend, Tyrone Perkins. . .
"a friend that sticks closer than a brother" (Proverbs 18:24).

And to

Otis, Paul and Neil, who immediately accepted me, although I
appeared a bit "pale."

TABLE OF CONTENTS

ACKNOWLEDGMENTS

I am deeply grateful to those who have helped make this book a reality.

Occasionally, God places a person in our life to help transform us into his Son's likeness and to abet us toward our destination. For me that person was Reverend Tyrone A. Perkins, pastor of Westside Bible Baptist Church (Trenton, New Jersey). Tyrone has been my confidant, prayer warrior, mentor, advisor, editor, and. . .incredible friend. . .." This book would never have come to print had it not been for Tyrone's countless hours of reading and rereading of the text to make corrections and suggestions.

Many thanks to Westside Bible Baptist who adopted me as one of their own, prayed for my ministry and spiritual growth, and demonstrated genuine Christlike love toward me.

Pastors Craig Garriott and Stan Long of Faith Christian Fellowship (Baltimore, MD) who took the time to sit with me, answer my questions, and share with transparency their struggles and journey as they pursued their reconciliation ministry in Pen Lucy and Baltimore.

Dr. Anthony Campolo who, despite the tremendous demands on his time and energy, found time to answer questions and recommend some essential reading to enhance the substance of this book.

I owe a special thanks to Pastor Chris Freet (Beach Lake Free Methodist Church, Beach Lake, PA) who surrendered his pulpit to me numerous times and opened his heart to assist in my ministry growth. Your mission statement of "Loving God. . .Loving Others" is the epitome of the two greatest commandments!

Finally, I would not have even attempted to write this book if it hadn't been for an exceptional woman who believed in me more than I believed in myself. A woman who looks past my sin and vulnerabilities to see a man she thinks is capable of greatness. Thank you for being patient all those hours I was consumed with research, reading and writing. I wish everyone had a person in their life who believed in them as much as you believe in me. Carolyn, your love for me has healed many wounds and your love for others is a testimony of how God has transformed your life.

INTRODUCTION

"Anyone, then, who knows the good he ought to do and doesn't do it, sins" (James 4:17).

First and foremost, this book is addressed to the white evangelical church in America; to all the congregants and adherents of those churches, not because only the white community has demonstrated apathy towards racial reconciliation (there is plenty of blame to go around!), but because as a Caucasian evangelical pastor, I am more qualified to address the white church than I am the churches of other ethnicities.

Unless you live like the oblivious ostrich, with your head in the sand, I'm sure you have seen and experienced the longstanding problem which, regrettably, has improved little over our national history: the racial segregation within America's evangelical church. For the life of me, I can't quite figure out why the majority of the American church still remains segregated. I know many absolutely wonderful Christians, both white and black, who worship in a church that refuses to take deliberate action towards making their church welcoming for people of color.

The subject of race in American society has been exhausted to the extent that most everyone cringes when the subject surfaces. Many white Americans have taken one extreme or another; to embrace political correctness (with little heartfelt initiative) and seek to exorcise the demon of "white guilt" in order to appease their consciences or, on the opposite polarity, accusing the African American community of using the "race card" to get unfair opportunities. Both attitudes are contrary to Christian reconciliation and detrimental to achieving any progress toward that goal within the church. Perhaps the real reason for corporate segregation within the church lies in the individual Christian's heart, that secret place that each of us hope will never be exposed.

The truth of the matter is that ethnic integration within the American church is pathetically inept. The king of deception, the prince of the power of the air, Satan himself, has deceived White American Christians to such a degree that most believe there *is no* racial problem in the church. The Apostle Paul warned of this type of deception within the church when he said, ". . . I am afraid that just as Eve was deceived by the serpent's cunning, your minds may somehow be led astray from your sincere and pure devotion to Christ" (2 Corinthians 11:3). Such an oblivious mindset is one that has permeated the church and has had a horrendous impact in countless ways, not just on racial reconciliation. The apathy that exists within the church is evidence enough of the serious nature, but one need only take a conscious look at the ethnic make-up within a 10 mile radius of their church and then look at the ethnic make-up *within* their church. Is it, at the very least, representative of that community? If not, why not?

It is a sad commentary that American secular society, as a whole, has progressed more toward racial reconciliation and has realized a more socially harmonious relationship between differing ethnic groups than the American evangelical church. Sadly, in many secular arenas of American life, unity and racial reconciliation are more prevalent than in Christian circles. Isn't it just like Satan to use the pagan world to embarrass Christians? But we are *not* embarrassed! That's the point! In the twisted manipulation of Satan, he takes something which is good, Christlike unity and true acceptance of ethnically diverse people, and uses it to show the unbelieving world that their actions are actually more "holy" than that of Christians! This only provides credence for those who point to the hypocrisy of the modern day (American) Christian. It is the synthetic presentation of Christ's love which disgusts the world because of its hypocrisy.

In the midst of the deceptive moral compromise we label as "political correctness," we get a glimpse of what could be. . .what *should be*. The difference is that much of what we see in our society is "tolerance" for others. What Christians should strive for is true unity, the product of a people who are compelled to express Christ's love to everyone. The two are quite different from each other. Tolerance is not motivated by love, but by the selfish pursuit of peace and harmony. The desired outcome is admirable, but the motive is not, and it will never achieve the utopia it so desperately wants. The definition of tolerance in our contemporary American society is one that advocates a mentality of universalism. It preaches a philosophy of subjective truth. Truth is relative, depending upon each individual's definition of the word and so, with this type of mentality, there is always an abundance of "truth" surrounding the world. Of course, when we stop and think about it, this philosophy is quite absurd! Reid Monaghan makes an acute observation by stating that "a plurality of contradicting truths is an impossibility."[1] Tolerance, when it encourages or sanctions sin (actions which are contrary to God's mandates and commandments clearly taught in the Scriptures), should be protested, but when it teaches an attitude of kinship and peace among all people, it should be gladly embraced.

Henri Nouwen reminds us that "In a world so torn apart by rivalry, anger, and hatred, we have the privileged vocation to be living signs of a love that can bridge all divisions and heal all wounds."[2] Whether the American church's sinful actions are deliberate or unintentional, my prayer is that this book might help to bring conviction and a change of heart, and encourage change within the evangelical faith in America. I pray that serious and honest dialogue occurs within the wonderfully diverse peoples that make-up this group. I hope that creative solutions surface by thinking outside the box, in new ways, rather than the shallow and faulty ways we have attempted futilely in the past.

Remember, all people are prejudiced, just as all of us are sinners. We have a tendency to view everything through the "me" filter which taints our perspective with selfishness. It is through the power of the Holy Spirit that we can expose our own sinful opinions and seek to love all people as our example, Christ, did. To excuse racism as something which lies within all humankind would be an attitude of both acceptance and apathy. Whether dormant or expressive, our prejudices toward people who appear different than us is something which needs to be exorcised and purged just as any sin should be, but turning a deaf ear and ignoring the reality of one's own heart is to ignore the prodding of the Holy Spirit who exposes sin.

I have deliberately avoided the use of the word "race," to describe people groups who may be distinguished by visible physical differences because it would be nothing more than buying into the social construct which has been created by our society. The American Anthropological Association in their "Statement on Race," noted that in the United States, more than any other country, the populace has been "conditioned to viewing human races as natural and separate divisions within the human species based on visible physical differences."[3] They go on to point out that "evidence from the analysis of genetics (e.g., DNA). . ..(reveals) that there is greater variation *within* "racial" groups than between them."[4]

In Thomas Phillip's television review of the PBS series *Race: The Power of an Illusion*, series creator Larry Adelman challenges the concept that "race" is at all meaningful. "'Skin color really is only skin deep,' Adelman insists. On the other hand, however, race remains an extremely important social construct. 'Just because race is meaningless as a biological construction doesn't mean that it has no meaning as a social construction,' Adelman warns. . .to recognize that 'race' is an illusion is not to deny the power of that illusion.'"[5] God only refers to one race, the human race. Any use of the word "race" for my purposes here would actually have the opposite effect that I am attempting to accomplish through this book. If we would stop and consider the reality of our similarities rather than our differences, we would certainly come to an agreement that there is only one race, the human race.

This book is not a "how to" book detailing various techniques or offering a 5 step program in multicultural acclimatization. There are plenty of wonderful books describing those much needed tools. This book is intended to be nothing more than a wake-up call, based on biblical truths, to churches and Christians who, intentionally or not, have turned a blind eye to the ethnic division realized in evangelical

America. This is a plea for all believers to evaluate their hearts and see if there is any (racialized) "wicked way" within themselves (Psalm 139:23-24). My prayer is that you will read this book with an open mind, and if so, your heart will follow.

Some who read this book will be offended. If this book offends because of the truths it speaks and the evil and sinful actions it exposes, then I am not apologetic. This book has been written with prayerful consideration and my heartfelt intent was to write the "truth in love" (Ephesians 4:15). If the truth offends you then it is not the messenger with whom you have an issue.

NOTES:

INTRODUCTION

[1] Ravi Zacharias, *Has Christianity Failed You?(* Grand Rapids: Zondervan, 2010), 59.

[2] Henri Nouwen, *Bread for the Journey* (New York: HarperOne, 1997), August 9.

[3] American Anthropological Association, "Statement on 'Race'" doc. on-line]; available from http://www.aaanet.org/stmts/racepp.htm; accessed 14 Mar. 2012.

[4] Ibid.

[5] Thomas E. Phillips, "Debunking the idea of Race," *Research News & Opportunities in Science and Theology,* May 2003, 16.

1

AN EVIL LURKING

Be very careful, then, how you live—not as unwise but as wise, making the most of every opportunity, because the days are evil.
Ephesians 5:15-16

If you search for good, you will find favor; but if you search for evil, it will find you! Proverbs 11:27

This is how we know who the children of God are and who the children of the devil are: Anyone who does not do what is right is not God's child, nor is anyone who does not love their brother and sister.
1 John 3:10-11

*E*VIL. The very word stirs our very soul and shakes our inner conscience. The word itself, and any connotation of the word in connection with the western (specifically the American) church, would quickly be viewed as inappropriate and misguided by many who consider themselves "Christians." But make no mistake; there is clearly an evil, disobedient wind that has blown through our open stained-glass windows permeating our pulpits and pews across our nation. This evil manifests itself in the cancerous growth of racism which has its deep roots within the "heart-set" of the American Christian and thus prevents reconciliation and widespread unity.

Certainly, the use of the word *evil* may seem extreme to some, but perhaps this disagreement may lie in how one defines the word. Theologians Wood and Marshall provide a thoughtful definition of the word evil in the New Bible Dictionary. They describe evil, and its relationship to sin, this way: "Evil has a broader meaning than SIN. The Hebrew word comes from a root meaning 'to spoil', 'to break in pieces'- being broken and so made worthless. It is essentially what is unpleasant, disagreeable, and offensive. The word binds together the evil deed and its consequences. In the New Testament the Greek words kakos and ponēros mean respectively the quality of evil in its essential character, and its hurtful effects or influence. It is used in both physical and moral senses. While these aspects are different, there is frequently a close relationship between them. Much physical evil is due to moral evil: suffering and sin are not necessarily connected in individual cases, but human selfishness and sin explain much of the world's ills."[1] Ravi

Zacharias defines evil as "that which puts self over every other person's right and essential worth."[2] If we accept these definitions of evil then it is no stretch to call the lack of ethnic reconciliation and integration within our churches, and the overall indifference within the American Evangelical Church, as evil.

It may, on the surface, sound like a bit of an exaggeration to label ethnic segregation within the church as evil, but the devaluing of another human *who is made in God's image*, is nothing less than a horror to God and we need to grasp this truth if we are to hope for any nationwide, spiritual change of heart. Why is it that we cannot picture ourselves as having anything to do with evil even though we are willing participants? Make no mistake, indifference, apathy, a lack of personal and local church responsibility, laziness, a lack of action and finger-pointing are all symptoms of a lurking evil which we are (consciously or not) encouraging. Yes, those of us who are in Christ have become "new creations" (1 Corinthians 5:17) and no, absolutely no one can "pluck us" out of God's hand (John 10:28-29), but what are we to say when some willingly leave their divine Love and stroll hand-in-hand with evil?

FINGER-POINTING

We certainly get our desire to blame someone else naturally enough. When Adam was confronted in the garden after he had disobeyed God and eaten the "red, juicy fruit," God asked him, "Have you eaten from the tree that I commanded you not to eat from?" (Genesis 3:11). Almost instinctively, Adam blames both God and Eve for his failure. "*The woman you put here with me*—she gave me some fruit from the tree, and I ate it" (v.12, emphasis mine). God then turns to Eve and asks her what she had done. Her response was exactly like Adam's, to blame someone else. "*The serpent deceived me*, and I ate" (v. 13). We are a chip off the old block! "It isn't my fault our church is not representative of the community that surrounds it. They can come here if they want. They are the ones who alienate themselves from us." We have all heard the various excuses and seen the self-righteous finger-pointing within our own churches and as a result, we live comfortably with the status quo.

SIN = DEATH

There are always consequences of sin. Sin always causes death. . .always! Adam and Eve's "primal act of folly. . .subjected the whole universe to the forces of decay and cosmic wickedness, and hence to the possibility of suffering and tragedy."[3] The contemporary church's sin of refusing to address the lack of racial and ethnic harmony is killing the unity that Jesus prayed to his Father for in The Gospel of John chapter 17. This unity should not be interpreted as exclusively for the local church, but also for the universal church, representing all believers throughout the world. Jesus knew that divisions and selfish desires would splinter the church and that the world would mock Christians for their hypocrisy and lack of unity. Perhaps that is one of the reasons why the percentage of atheists and agnostics in America has more than doubled since 1990.[4] The world is sickened by Christians who don't practice what they preach. This selfish mentality is not the testimony that should be contagious, creating an environment by which Christ is honored and a lost world hungers to be a part. What we are selling, the world does not want to buy. The world has enough hatred and bigotry. We preach that "God so loved the world," but live a life practicing that only some in the world are worthy of our love. We need this sin to be exposed and to discern the situation for what it is, a longstanding problem which has had devastating consequences. Without acknowledging that we are part of the problem, we play into Satan's hand of deceiving ourselves of truth, resulting in an absence of repentance and an apathetic attitude towards turning from our sin.

THE REALIZATION
THAT A PROBLEM EXISTS

The Book of James has been much maligned for a variety of reasons, by a variety of theologians, from Martin Luther to Martin Dibelius, yet it is an extremely practical book, filled with ethical teaching. It is direct and straightforward, needing little interpretation from the reader. It is a book that David Nystrom describes as having been written to address problems that a church was experiencing, "including divisiveness, intolerance, favoritism, and the overpowering desire for wealth and status."[5] These problems, or more accurately, these "sins," are eerily similar to what the contemporary Western church struggles with today and which hampers true reconciliation between the people of various skin color.

In the introduction to his commentary on the Book of James, Nystrom writes: "On January 1, 1990, President Václav Havel of Czechoslovakia addressed his nation. It had been a few weeks since his country peaceably ousted the Communist totalitarian government that had held power for forty years. Only two days before, Havel had been elected President by a parliament still dominated by Communists. Havel said:

> We live in a contaminated moral environment. . . We learned not to believe in anything, to ignore each other, to care only for ourselves. Concepts such as love, friendship, compassion, humility, and forgiveness lost their depth and dimensions, and for many of us they came to represent only psychological peculiarities, or to resemble long-lost greetings from ancient times. . . When I talk about contaminated moral atmosphere. . .I am talking about us. . . Why do I say this? It would be quite unreasonable to understand the sad legacy of the last forty years as something alien, something bequeathed to us by some distant relative. On the contrary, we must accept this legacy as a sin we committed against ourselves.

There are many points of similarity between this brief excerpt from Havel's speech and the letter of James. Havel writes from the heart, and like James his is a heart that has known adversity as well as joy. Both are keen observers of human nature. Both are vitally interested in the creation of true community, a community marked by mutual care and interdependent responsibility. In an era in which a sense of personal responsibility seems endangered, Havel calls it true. James also is unafraid to call sin by its true name, and like Havel he will not allow us to shirk responsibility for our own actions, or for the evil that occurs because of our inaction."[6]

"Ninety percent of African-American Christians worship in all-black churches. Ninety percent of white American Christians worship in all-white churches,' said Chris Rice, coauthor of *More Than Equals: Racial Healing for the Sake of the Gospel*." ". . .Years since the incredible victories of the civil rights movement, we continue to live in the trajectory of racial fragmentation. The biggest problem is that we don't see that as a problem."[7] This is the most disturbing obstacle in the white church; this perception that there is no problem of ethnic relations within the faith. A concern I have is now that a black man has reached the pinnacle of success in America by reaching the White House, many whites will be deluded into believing that equality among blacks and whites has been achieved. Being oblivious to the problem and by not addressing it, the church has slipped into a perilous state. Just as Eve was deceived into disobedience, the church is also being induced to believing that their sinful actions are acceptable. The Apostle Paul tells the Corinthian church that they were being seduced into disobedience by Satan just as Eve was (2 Corinthians 11: 2-4). By getting sucked into the lie the church demonstrates disloyalty to Christ. Ignorance is no excuse for Christian inaction, for when it comes to obedience and a life of action, Christians should be without hesitation or compromise. Believers have the gift of the indwelling Holy Spirit and, if attentive to his wisdom and discernment, will see deception for what it truly is.

NON-ACTION

In his first letter to the Corinthians, the Apostle Paul chastises the congregation for yielding more to the spirit of this world than to the Spirit of God. The purpose of his letter was to teach the church at Corinth what a church is supposed to be like and why it is to be this way. It is a message that the church in America needs desperately to hear today. Paul emphasizes that the church needs to be holy, pure, united and loving. In chapter 5 he admonishes the church for allowing sin to fester. A man in their midst was having a sexual relationship with his stepmother and the Corinthians ignored and tolerated the sinful practice. As a result, they failed at one of the primary purposes of the church, to teach how to live as godly people (Titus 2:11-12). When sin is tolerated, unity suffers. Unity dies as a result of allowing sin to grow terminally. The sin of prejudice, the indifference toward fellow believers of differing colors, and the deliberate refusal to turn from these sins has caused a lack of unity with the American evangelical church. Paul could have been addressing contemporary American churches when he says, "How terrible that you should boast about your spirituality, and yet you let this sort of thing go on. Don't you realize that if even one person is allowed to go on sinning, soon all will be affected?" (5:6-7 NLT).

So soon we forget. The contemporary American Christian has had a memory lapse, forgetting when we were aliens to Christ, instead of experiencing the acceptance of family; we were on the outside looking in. There was a time when we were searching for meaning and substance in our lives. We were not part of the family of Christ, yet in our ignorance we longed for this belonging and acceptance which could only be found in Christ. Now, through the gradual numbing of church exclusivity, we have committed a sin which has both a gradual and long-term effect. It is time to take off the blinders and unmask the evil, calling it what it is - divisive prejudice. We must expose the division and restrictedness, conscious or not, that is rotting our moral fabric of unity within the American Evangelical church. When the church is not doing the work of Christ, it has failed in its mission! She is to bring Good News to the poor, freedom to the oppressed and joy to the afflicted.[8]

The personal and deliberate expression of racism is not quite as obvious as it was 40 (or 100) years ago, but the symptoms and their consequences are rampant and are quietly having a terminal effect on the church's Christly influence in the world in which it exists. Our godly influence in a world desperate for peace and love has lost its potency. . . .and there is plenty of blame to go around. This is not only a problem with the "white" church. There is a mindset of separatism in non-white congregations as well.

If the church is an, albeit imperfect, preview of what heaven will look like, I'm not all that excited about going there. Sarcasm aside, the truth is that the American Christian church has been lulled into a sleepy existence which is reflected in their lack of action involving ethnic reconciliation. They have been deceived and manipulated into believing that any and all segregation in the local church is simply a reflection of the different cultural worship styles and preferences of people of "different" colors.

I once was a member of a nondenominational (evangelical) church in suburban Philadelphia which drew in excess of 900 worshipers on any given Sunday (I understand that today they exceed 2200 worshippers on Sunday mornings). The preaching was sound, the music was wonderful and they attempted (and were quite successful) to make this church a place where seekers would feel comfortable and thus, hear the gospel preached. Out of those 900 people, 4 were African American, and of those 4, 2 were Nigerian with PhDs! Those blacks (including those who are first generation African Americans) are more widely accepted within the white church than those who were born in the United States largely because they associate themselves more with the white establishment than the African-American culture, partly because of their high education level and that their workplace and communities tend to be dominated by whites. It appears as though they have chosen to embrace white culture and values and to reject African American culture and values.

In an attempt to be relevant within the community in which it stands, this church was oblivious to the many people of color that surrounded them. When I asked one of the pastoral staff why there was such a lack of ethnic diversity within our church I was told that there was no African Americans within the 10 mile radius of the church, yet I find it interesting that a good percentage of the white congregants drive in excess of 10 miles, driving past black and Hispanic neighborhoods to attend this specific church. It is always easy to find excuses why not to step out in faith. We can always justify our inaction and find support for our preconceived mindset built on a lack of facts. Churches should understand their market, those people they are trying to attract within a certain circumference of where their church building is located. In this age of internet access to information it is not difficult for one to find out the ethnic make-up of their community.

The suffocating passivity and non-action with which the American Evangelical church has displayed its attempts at ethnic reconciliation is nothing short of pathetic. Christians who are blind to the lack of unity within the Church are people whose faith is manipulated and manufactured by superficial leaders and whose impact for Christ is marginal at best. Their expectation is that this is someone else's problem to fix. It is this type of delusion which allows them to believe that they are not indifferent or prejudice. These same people may be those who volunteer for short-term mission trips to the inner city to work among African Americans. Their experience provides a realistic taste of both the problem that exists and even creates a bridge-building initiation, but as soon as they return to their safe, homogenized lives, the thoughts and ideas that stirred within them are forgotten. These experiences could be opportunities to bring change within the local church. Bestselling author and speaker Tony Campolo adds, "On the other hand, if they begin to get involved with people in their own immediate neighborhoods, the engagement will not be simply for a couple of weeks, such as short-term mission experiences provide, but will require ongoing, daily connectedness with these persons. In short, those who are in need in their own neighborhoods will have to become part of their everyday lives, and that will lead to them encroaching on the normative lifestyles that the white congregants generally experience."[9]

Mega churches that have congregations numbering in the thousands have done a much better job of integrating a multiethnic congregation. They should be praised for their progress in this area, but in a mass assembly it's much easier to integrate "color" into an existing white congregation. It is much more difficult to create an ethnic mix within small groups which have, obviously, a much more intimate and communicative environment. When groups of 10 or less gather, there is a greater sense of intimacy, interaction, and transparency simply because all three of these characteristics are a prerequisite for small groups to prosper. Statistics show that 59% of the churches in America have between 7 and 99 congregants/adherents.[10] It is in these churches that segregation thrives.

It has been said that all that is necessary for evil to triumph is for good men (and women) to do nothing. If this is true, then the contemptible unresponsiveness in the American Evangelical church is allowing evil to propagate in the very drywall of our sanctuaries and it is rotting the framework in which it stands. If there is anyone who should stand against evil and do anything and everything to prevent its acceptance, it is the church. It is the church that can and should initiate change through love. It is inactivity that lies at the root of our sin. It is slothfulness which prevents any passion for doing what is right. ". . .whatever is true, whatever is noble, whatever is right, whatever is pure, whatever is lovely, whatever is admirable—if anything is excellent or praiseworthy—think about such things" (Philippians 4:8). And act upon it.

The Church missed an excellent opportunity to take the leadership regarding reconciliation during the civil rights movement of the 1960's, but it didn't. Martin Luther King realized that it is the Church that should show the nation (and the world) what diversity in unity can look like. When asked if it wasn't the Christian Church where integration could only be truly realized and modeled and thus the true Christ-like heart of Christians would be exemplified to society, Dr. King said:

> As a preacher. . .I must admit that I have gone through those moments when I was greatly disappointed with the church and what it has done in this period of social change. We must face the fact that in America, the church is still the most segregated major institution in America. At 11:00 on Sunday morning when we stand and sing and Christ has no east or west, we stand at the most segregated hour in this nation. This is tragic. Nobody of honesty can overlook this. Now, I'm sure that if the church had taken a stronger stand all along, we wouldn't have many of the problems that we have. The first way that the church can repent, the first way that it can move out into the arena of social reform is to remove the yoke of segregation from its own body. Now, I'm not saying that society must sit down and wait on a spiritual and moribund church as we've so often seen. I think it should have started in the church, but since it didn't start in the church, our society needed to move on. The church, itself, will stand under the judgment of God. Now that the mistake of the past has been made, I think that the opportunity of the future is to really go out and to transform American society,

and where else is there a better place than in the institution that should serve as the moral guardian of the community. The institution that should preach brotherhood and make it a reality within its own body.[11]

Dr. King made this statement in an interview in 1963. How pathetically little progress the American Church has made in the past (nearly) 50 years! It has been preoccupied with programs, and events, and entertaining relativism to fill the pews, all the while ignoring the basics of Christianity. James and Lillian Breckenridge accurately expose this in their book; *What Color is Your God?* "We have fascinated ourselves with spiritual promises and become pre-occupied with 'the blessed hope' of Christ's coming. In the midst of programs, buildings, and prosperity we have forgotten one simple fact – we are sinners. We have failed to repent of our national sin of racism. It is time for a 'baptism of repentance' in which we recognize the true spirituality of Christianity."[12]

Although King is credited for the quote "Eleven o'clock Sunday morning is the most segregated hour in America," Kevin D. Hendricks noted that "while King frequently used the line, he was actually quoting a 1950s Reader's Digest article on racism written by Billy Graham. Graham took an early and strong stand for civil rights, insisting on holding integrated crusades in Jackson, Miss., as early as 1952 (two years before the landmark Brown v. Board of Education case). During a 1953 crusade in Chattanooga, Tenn., Billy Graham himself tore down ropes dividing white and black sections."[13]

DOESN'T GOD CARE?

No one would argue that there has been a significant decline in the moral fabric of America. We call ourselves a godly nation but we are the largest exporter of pornography, we abort well over 2 million children every year, and our violence against each other is occurring at an alarming rate. We in the church pray for peace and healing and for the lost to find the everlasting light that can only come from a personal relationship with Jesus Christ, and yet it seems as though our prayers fall on deaf ears. Is God listening? Doesn't he care what is happening in this great country? Are we not a blessed nation; his "chosen" people? After all, we sing God Bless America at every ball game!

American Christian patriots must place their allegiance first to the cross, then to their country. Nationalism should not be greater than "Christism." After all, this country (and world) is *not* our home. Somehow through the years we've gotten that order confused. The writer of Hebrews mentions four Old Testament heroes that had their eyes fixed on their real nationality, the one from above. In chapter 11 we read, "All these people were still living by faith when they died. They did not receive the things promised; they only saw them and welcomed them from a distance, admitting that they were foreigners and strangers on earth. People who say such things show that they are looking for a country of their own. If they had been thinking of the country they had left, they would have had opportunity to return. Instead, *they were longing for a better country*—a heavenly one. Therefore God is not ashamed to be called their God, for he has prepared a city for them" (vv. 13-16, italics mine). I served in the United States Navy for 5 years and would have gladly given my life so that others could live in freedom, and I deeply appreciate those who have served and those who gave the ultimate sacrifice so that we can worship our Lord and Savior without fear of persecution, but my deepest passion and dedication is not to any earthly kingdom. There's an old song entitled, "This World is Not My Home." One stanza goes something like this:

This World Is Not My Home, I'm Just a Passing Thru
My Treasures Are Laid Up, Somewhere Beyond the Blue
The Angels Beckon Me From Heaven's Open Door
And I Can't Feel At Home In This World Anymore."

When we view the bigger picture, that *all* of God's elect will sing praises to Jesus Christ, hand-in-hand, knee-by-knee, our perspective on our brothers and sisters of color should change. Our calloused hearts will be softened and we will feel the conviction of our lack of love for others.

So, is God listening to our prayers? There is a trio of verses in the Bible which may very well explain why our prayers are not being answered. Prayers which we know are God's will as much as ours. The Psalmist tells us to "take delight in the Lord, and he will give you the desires of your heart" (Psalm 37:4). We quickly remember the second part of that verse, the part that gives us want we want, but ignore the preface. What does it mean to "take delight in the Lord?" One who trusts in the Lord and has *righteous* desires is one who finds joy in the Lord. That brings us to the second of the three verses. James tells us to ". . . confess your sins to each other and pray for each other so that you may be healed. The prayer of a righteous man is powerful and effective" (5:16). Spiritual healing is imperative before we can be "right" with God. Sin is a self-made barrier that hinders our prayer life, which is why we should always confess our sins to God *before* we reach the point of supplication (requesting). Like a spoiled child, many of us pray "Gimme, gimme, gimme," without first humbling ourselves and seeking God's will rather than our own.

The final verse (s) is once again found in the Psalms, chapter 139 verses 23 and 24. This passage gives us the prelude to answered prayer. The Psalmist understands that he must be right with God before he will be given the desires of his heart. "Search me, God, and know my heart; test me and know my anxious thoughts. See if there is any offensive (wicked/evil) way in me, and lead me in the way everlasting" (parenthesis mine). Could it be that the American evangelical church's corporate prayers have been less effective because of their corporate sin? Could it be that the revival that this country so desperately needs is slow to happen because those who want it the most are preventing the spiritual progress? Friends, the church needs to get on its knees, repent, and ask for both healing and empowerment. If we are averting reconciliation, let us ask for forgiveness and take action, empowered by the Holy Spirit, and show the secular world that Christ's love is potent and able to unravel centuries of hatred and alienation.

I believe that America, in general, and the evangelical church, more specifically, is at a crucial crossroad in its history. The moral decline of our society is clear all around us. Perhaps the most obvious indication of our spiritual and ethical decay is what has been allowed to air on television and what shows are the most popular. Shows like "Jersey Shore" and "Housewives of Beverly Hills/Atlanta/Orange County/West Chester County/New Jersey" are wildly popular as they celebrate a life of sexual promiscuity, substance abuse and crude language. As Christians we have been consecrated, "set apart," for God's good purpose. When the church accepts sin, either consciously or subconsciously, we stunt its spiritual growth and prevent God's blessings upon it. Make no mistake, just as the Great Shepherd leaves the 99 sheep to pursue and find that one lost lamb (Luke 15:1-7), so too will God seek the church which has lost its way. He will do *anything* to bring it back to his fold, even if that means allowing it to go through great adversity. What God requires is a "broken and contrite heart"(Psalm 51:17) and if we are going to turn away from our sin of apathy and indifference as it applies to ethnic unity, we must acknowledge the need for corporate confession and seek God's restoration.

CANCEROUS SIN

I see a parallel between the church's sin and King David's, as told in 2 Samuel. The Bible tells us that David was a man who pleased God. In Acts 13:22 we read that "After removing Saul, he (God) made David their king. God testified concerning him: 'I have found David son of Jesse, a man after my own heart; he will do everything I want him to do." But one day David became selfish and wanted what was not his. He made a critical decision with no regard for others. He committed adultery and then in an attempt to cover it up, he committed murder. In a penitential Psalm (Psalm 51) we see a man who has been crushed spiritually. David pleads for forgiveness and cleansing (vv. 1-2), confesses his sin and acknowledges his guilt (vv. 3-6), asks God for restoration and pardon (vv. 7-12), decides to turn to God and offer heartfelt praise (vv. 13-17), and prays for the future of Jerusalem and God's favor toward it (vv. 18-19). God heard his prayer! This is exactly what the American Evangelical church must do.

The evil I am speaking about originates in the selfishness of the church by its constant looking inward rather that outward. That is what the world does; it is always motivated by selfish desires. James rebukes the church for squandering God's blessings on themselves (James 4:3) which caused quarrels, conflict and division among them. He appropriately calls them adulterers because we, the church, are Christ's bride (Ephesians 5:25-27), and when we look elsewhere for our joy and needs we fail to honor him and turn to an illegitimate relationship with the world in order to be satisfied. "You adulteresses, do you not know that friendship with the world is hostility toward God?" (4:4). James goes on to suggest the cure for their illness. He says they must "submit" and "draw near to God" (vv. 7-8), "cleanse" their hands and "purify" their hearts (v.8), mourn over their sin (v.9), and "humble" themselves "in the presence of God" (v. 10). Humility is the opposite of pride. Pride is selfishness, humility is self- *less*-ness.

In Bruce Milne's excellent book, "Know the Truth," there is a succinct explanation of sin and its relationship to one's neighbor. "Sin brings *conflict* and produces the great divisions of humankind. It causes racial prejudice and antagonism. It contributes to demonic forms of nationalism. . . .It creates social divisions and so leads to group and class conflict; it separates the 'haves' from the 'have-nots'. It causes conflicts within all human groups, whether educational, community, social leisure or religious. It divides families and churches. Paradoxically, the threat posed by our neighbor often makes us run for security into sometimes unlikely and unhealthy alliances."[14] Sin always causes death, and in the case of relationships it has rippling and long-term effects. In the case of the United States we have seen generational prejudice, poverty and crime for a period of several centuries. Sin has a contagious effect, especially among the spiritually immature. It is a cancer which requires spiritual surgery to be removed. Perhaps it is heart surgery that we really need, for it is the heart that makes men unclean. ". . .out of the heart come evil thoughts—murder, adultery, sexual immorality, theft, false testimony, slander" (Matthew 15:29).

Sin is evil in practice. The human (sinful) psyche has an uncanny ability to justify sin and to minimize its horror. In the sterile environment of many American churches, we all look pretty good. . .pretty righteous. We comb our hair and put on our Sunday best and smile and sing and say the right things. Who in this group could ever be called prejudiced? If we could only look into the hearts of these moralistic people I wonder what we would see. "The Lord does not look at the things people look at. People look at the outward appearance, but the Lord looks at the heart" (1 Samuel 16:7b). What is it that God sees in your heart? Does he see the genuine unselfish love for others? Does he see a heart desire to put others' needs before you own? Does he see the loving desire to bring people of diverse backgrounds together in Christian unity? Does he see someone who looks at others as Jesus did, or does he see a hardened heart, one that judges and condemns those who are different from us?

LEARNING FROM HISTORY

Evil best manifests itself when one's heart is hardened. The word used in Scripture for a" hardened" heart is probably better translated *callous* or *petrified*. The connotation is that something that was once soft has been made hard, like petrified wood that, over time, has been transformed into a substance as hard as rock. The story of John Newton is a beautiful example of how God penetrates the hardened heart to accomplish righteousness. There are few people, Christians or secularists alike, who have not heard the sweet sound of the hymn "Amazing Grace." It is a somewhat autobiographical song by the self-proclaimed wretch, John Newton. Born in London, England in 1725, Newton sailed the Mediterranean with his father and later, while at a young age of 19, was pressed into military service upon the warship H.M.S. Harwich. It wasn't long after that the young Newton realized the unpleasant living conditions typical of eighteenth century nautical life and deserted, only to be captured, publically flogged and promptly placed back aboard the miserable ship. He was demoted from midshipman to common seaman (I once was a common seaman and believe me, there's nothing pretty about being one!).

Desperate to find an alternative vessel, Newton thought his luck had changed when he was placed on a slave ship headed to the coast of Sierra Leone, but conditions on that ship were even worse. He was a servant to a slave trader who was not a stranger to abusing both slaves and hired hands alike. A few years later he was rescued by a sea captain who knew his father and, as fate would have it, eventually became the captain of his own slave ship. Newton not only saw nothing wrong with the evils of forced bondage, he made a living kidnapping and transporting the slaves.

While on the merchant ship Greyhound, Newton found himself in a torrid storm off the coast of Donegal. His ship took on significant water so that he wondered whether there was the slightest chance he would not perish. There's an old "sea-saying" that goes something like, "There are no atheists on a ship in the middle of a hurricane." Newton awoke in the middle of the night to discover the ship rapidly filling with water. Crying out to God, and hoping there was such a Divine Being, he begged for deliverance. After his desperate call, cargo floated past him and clogged the hole where the water was coming in, enabling the ship to drift to safety. On the way home to England, John read the Bible daily and on March 10, 1748 he turned his life over to Christ. His conversion included, as it should, his turning from sin and embracing mercy and justice.

> Amazing Grace, how sweet the sound,
> That saved a wretch like me. . ..
> I once was lost but now am found,
> Was blind, but now, I see.

I tell this story to illustrate the power one person can have when they turn from evil and allow God to work in their life. Newton did not just turn away from the slave trade, he became a minister, hymn-writer, and later a protuberant supporter of the abolition of slavery. He was the author of many hymns, including "Amazing Grace" and "Glorious Things of Thee are Spoken." Jesus Christ is in the business of transforming lives. When we are willing to be obedient to him, miraculous things are accomplished. If one man had this much influence upon the church, just imagine what the American church could accomplish when they are committed to living a life honoring to Christ and empowered by the Holy Spirit!

When Jesus ascended into heaven he promised that the Holy Spirit, the Third Person of the Triune God, would be sent to be a helper to all of us who are disciples of Christ. Our Heavenly Father also gave us the Bible, God's Word as an incredible gift for us so that we would have hope (Romans 15:4), be offered wisdom for salvation through Jesus Christ, and to teach us righteousness that we may do good works. In the Apostle Paul's Second Letter to Timothy (3:15-18), he says, ". . . from infancy you have known the holy Scriptures, which are able to make you wise for salvation through faith in Christ Jesus. All Scripture is God-breathed and is useful for teaching, rebuking, correcting and training in righteousness, so that the man of God may be thoroughly equipped for every good work." God's Word also gives us the life stories of various people, specifically his chosen people, the Jews, to teach, rebuke, correct and train us by using their mistakes as examples of what we should not do.

Israel, God's chosen people, was notorious for disobeying and ignoring God's commands. Frequently throughout the historical and prophetic books we read the phrase, "again they did evil in the sight of the Lord." Throughout the Old Testament we see a cyclical pattern of the Israelites turning away from God, experiencing turmoil and hardship, crying out to the Lord for help, repenting of their sins and finally, being restored into a relationship with God. Throughout the book of Judges there is a sub-theme of Israel breaking their covenant with Yahweh (God). Israel's sin was her defection from, or forsaking of, the Lord, by worshiping idols and intermarrying with pagan (evil) nations. As much as God loved the Jewish nation, he punished them severely. God's anger is realized as he responds to Israel's spiritual adultery. In some cases they are sold into slavery. In others, they are defeated and plundered by opposing armies. In still others they had to hide themselves in caves and mountain clefts (6:1-6).

In the 17th chapter of 2 Kings we read about the fall of Israel. How in the world could the privileged nation which had God's favor fall so far and fast? The short answer is that they did evil in the sight of the Lord. They were once an obedient nation with a desire to please God, but they turned away from what they knew to be true and reaped God's condemnation upon themselves. Although

America is surely reaping the consequences of its godless ways, I don't believe we have seen God's full retribution. There may be a time of improvement, as in the case of Israel, before full judgment is realized, for there is often calm before the storm.

How is it that we can read the Bible and it not have a profound effect on our lives? Of course, I'm assuming that the Bible *is* read by Christians. Perhaps that is where one of our problems lies. Mission America Coalition recently published a revealing statistic stating that 65% of professing Christians in America do not read the Bible.[15] If the truth be known, that 65% is probably a very conservative number. A proper reading of the Bible requires three things: the Holy Spirit's illuminating work, the ability of the reader to interpret and discern what they are reading, and the desire to apply that which is read. I am convinced that if American Christians would return to daily reading and study of the Holy Scriptures our country would experience a spiritual revival!

I am not suggesting that most believers consciously or purposely support, or are proponents of, segregation within the church. What I am saying here is that by taking no action and/or ignoring the need to achieve true unity within the church, we are actually nurturing division. Division does not equal unity. If you find yourself nodding your head in agreement to what you are reading, why then are you doing nothing about it? Don't fall into the false mentality that there is nothing one person can do to help rectify this problem. When Christians see someone spearheading a righteous cause or concern they are quick to jump on the bandwagon and lend a helping hand. As in all of society, followers are plentiful, leaders are few. So, let me ask you a question. If you saw a brother or sister about to be blindsided by a truck they didn't see coming, would you pull them to safety? Of course you would. Why? Simply because it would be the right thing to do. Would it be evil to sit by and watch them be leveled by the oncoming truck? Why is doing nothing to promote ethnic harmony any different?

We know little about the prophet Micah whose Old Testament book bears his name. His name is apparently a shortened version of the name "Micaiah, which means "Who is like Yahweh?"[16] He began each message with the exhortation for the people of the nation to "listen" to what the Lord has to say. We, too, would do well to listen. "He has shown you, O mortal, what is good. And what does the LORD require of you? To act justly and to love mercy and to walk humbly with your God" (Micah 6:8). We have been called to turn from every evil practice which hinders unity among all of our brothers and sisters, whatever the color of their skin or the language they speak. We are to be actively working towards the manifestation of the Kingdom of God and that includes mercy and justice.

Micah was telling the nation that a right and beneficial relationship with God "involves three things: that individuals (a) act justly (be fair in their dealings with others), (b) love mercy. . .(carry through on their commitments to meet other's needs), and (c) walk humbly with. . .God (fellowship with Him in modesty, without arrogance)."[17] This should have been nothing new to the children of Israel because God had given these instructions to them through Moses.

Like those in Micah's day, many Christians today are not being just (Micah 2:1-2; 3:1-3; 6:11) by failing to demonstrate love to those whom they are called to serve. They are not dedicated to creating harmonious relationships with all believers. Listen to what God said these people were doing to fellow Israelites; "Lately my people have risen up like an enemy. You strip off the rich robe from those who pass by without a care, like men returning from battle. You drive the women of my people from their pleasant homes. You take away my blessing from their children forever." (Micah 2:8-9). This sounds eerily like what the white church is doing to African American brothers and sisters by ignoring their value and refusing to seek deliberate and meaningful relationships with them. Like the Israelites, African Americans are *God's people* towards whom we have been indifferent.

Can you picture the impact the church would have on our world if we actually practiced what we preach? Really! It would be nothing short of awe-inspiring! Let's wake up and come together in numbers to make a real difference. Let's be Christ-honoring by stepping out in faith, turning from the past sins we have practiced, and make a powerful statement to the world by our loving actions to all of God's creations. It is time for change. There is an evil lurking within the white church and it is time for repentance and change. The silence must stop! We must pray a prayer of reconciliation.

Father, God,

If we have sinned against our brother and sister, then we have sinned against you. You have told us in your Word that sin is anything which is contrary to your nature and character. Expose our sin, I pray. If we have become numb to spiritual sensitivity, then create a stimulus we cannot ignore, dear Lord. Cauterize our hearts and make us pure. Awaken us to any sin which is hindering your Spirit's work of unity in the church so that we may live in obedience and renewal.

In Jesus precious name we pray, Amen.

NOTES:

CHAPTER 1: AN EVIL LURKING

[1]   D. R. W. Wood and I. H. Marshall, *New Bible Dictionary,* 3d ed. (Leicester, England: Downers Grove, Ill.: InterVarsity Press, 1996), 348.

[2]   Zacharias, Has Christianity Failed You

[3]   Bruce Milne, "*Know the Truth,*" 3d ed. (Downers Grove, Il.: IVP Academic, 2009), 111.

[4]   Barry A. Kosmin and Ariela Keysar, *American Religious Identification Survey.* Document on-line. Available from http://commons.trincoll.edu/aris/files/2011/08/ARIS_Report_2008.pdf; accessed 2 Feb. 2012.

[5]   David P. Nystrom, *James,* The NIV Application Commentary, (Grand Rapids: Zondervan, 1997), 15.

[6]   Ibid.

[7]   About.com, "Ending Racial Segregation in the American Church by Promoting Diversity" [doc. on-line]; available from http://racerelations.about.com/od/diversitymatters/a/RacialSegregationinChurch.htm; accessed 21 Aug 2012.

[8]   1971 Synod of Bishops, "Justice in the World" [doc. on-line]; available from http://www.shc.edu/theolibrary/resources/synodjw.htm; accessed 5 March 2012.

[9]   Tony Campolo, interview by author, 12 Feb. 2013, email held by author.

[10]   Hartford Institute for Religion Research, "Fast Facts" [doc. on-line]; available from http://hirr.hartsem.edu/research/fastfacts/fast_facts.html; accessed 14 March 2012.

[11]   Healthy Diversity, "The Most Segregated Hour in America" [doc. on-line]; available from http://artlucero.wordpress.com/tag/most-segregated-hour-in-america/; accessed 9 Jan. 2012.

[12]   James and Lillian Breckenridge, *What Color is Your God,* (Grand Rapids: Baker Books, 2003), 11.

[13]   BillySpot, "Martin Luther King Jr. & Billy Graham" http://www.billyspot.com/martin-luther-king-jr-billy-graham/; accessed 26 Jun. 2012.

[14]   Milne, *Know the Truth,* 144.

[15]   Mission America, Coalition "Research and Trends" [doc. on-line]; available from http://www.missionamerica.org: accessed 11 Apr. 2012.

[16] John a Martin, *The Bible Knowledge Commentary*, *Micah*, eds., John F. Walvoord & Roy B. Zuck (Wheaton, Il.: Victor Books, 1985), 1475.

[17] Ibid., 1489.

2

DIVIDED AND CONQUERED

(THE DYSFUNCTIONAL EVANGELICAL FAMILY)

How good and pleasant it is when God's people live together in unity! Psalm 133:1

Is Christ divided? 1 Corinthians 1:13a

May the God who gives endurance and encouragement give you the same attitude of mind toward each other that Christ Jesus had, so that with one mind and one voice you may glorify the God and Father of our Lord Jesus Christ. Romans 15:5-7

*M*ost all of us have either heard of, or experienced firsthand, the pain and heartache that accompanies church division. Besides having long-term negative effects on the congregation, it sends a message to the secular world that if we cannot seem to get along with brothers and sisters *within* the church, how in the world can we be expected to get along with anyone *outside* the church? Splits in the church are most always the result of sin, corporately and/ or individually, which then fractures the body. What should never be overlooked is that any disunity within the church deeply grieves our Lord and Savior. A lack of unity within the church is much like a dysfunctional family, where conflicts, misbehavior, and the enabling of sinful practices are allowed to take root and to persist. Often the next generation (the children of the adult congregants) either grows up in the church with the understanding that these divisive actions are normal and acceptable, or worse, they become disgusted with the hypocrisy and hatred they see and leave the church in search of "greener" pastures. It is the cancer of disunity within the American Evangelical church, the lack of unity between ethnic groups, that we get the title for this book; *The Schism*. The noun *schisma* is a Greek word that means "division" and is used in the New Testament, mostly in 1 Corinthians, where Paul was exasperated by a lack of unity in the early church. Martyn Lloyd-Jones observed that people within the church who agreed about the centralities of the faith were dividing and separating from one another over matters that were not essential to salvation; not absolutely vital. "This is always one of the dangers afflicting us as evangelicals. We can be so rigid, so over-strict, and so narrow that we become guilty of schism."[1]

Corinth was a church divided. Chloe's friends or relatives informed Paul that there were problems within the church. "I appeal to you, brothers and sisters, in the name of our Lord Jesus Christ, that all of you agree with one another in what you say and that there be no divisions among you, but that you be perfectly united in mind and thought" (1 Corinthians 1:10). In explaining this verse, David K. Lowery shares that it is Christ who unites all Christians, regardless of their obvious, but *insignificant* differences. "This is the 10th reference to Christ in the first 10 verses, leaving no doubt as to the One Paul believed should be the source and focus of Corinthian unity. His appeal was for harmony, not the elimination of diversity. He desired a unity of all the parts, like a quilt of various colors and patterns blended together in a harmonious whole."[2] Paul could very well have been addressing the American church today. Sadly, instead of a harmonious unity, the church's fiber has remained unwoven as a result of ethnic segregation.

It is the work of the cross which unites believers together. Jesus' atoning work on the cross enabled the coming of the Holy Spirit. The Spirit's presence and power unites each believer to the body of Christ (1 Corinthians 12:13). If we listen to the (not so subtle) voice of God, we can hear Him calling throughout the Body of Christ today. He is calling for unity. He's calling us to lay down our disagreements and come together in preparation for Jesus' return. In the preface to his book *Love Covers*, Paul Billheimer exposes the sin of disunity and its disastrous effects. "The most important, momentous, crucial, but the most ignored, neglected, and unsolved problem that has faced the Church from its infancy to the present throbbing moment is the problem of disunity. The continuous and widespread fragmentation of the Church has been the scandal of the ages. It has been Satan's master strategy. The sin of disunity probably has caused more souls to be lost than all other sins combined."[3]

DISILLUSIONED REALITY

The American church has failed in its mission and purpose. . .period! While morphing into a tabernacle which seeks to be relevant to today's believer and seeker by incorporating audio-visual arts, contemporary music (complete with a rock band), and a more relaxed environment with no dress code, we have ignored the elementary requirement of community unity. I salute the creative efforts of local churches that strive to become more relevant and welcoming to those who find traditional or liturgical services to be outdated. However, when entertaining becomes a substitute for the preaching of God's Word that "Christ is Lord," the church has lost its clarity of purpose and mission. The increasingly popular "feel good" theology which refuses to preach truths that convict the heart, but instead create congregations that "feel good" (emotionally) about themselves, has resulted in a society of "Stagnant Christians" who are deceived into ignoring the sin which prevents spiritual growth and obedience, resulting in maturity. One finds genuine unity where there is a hunger for biblical preaching, heartfelt confession, and a true selflessness motivated by love. The dichotomy between God's definition of unity and the current segregation within the American Evangelical church is a dirty little secret carefully crafted by the man-made barrier that keeps us proud in our mono-ethnic churches as we obliviously bang head-on into our church walls like bumper cars at an amusement park. We are confined within these walls of the church with a false sense of security and the impression that we have created the "perfect" church. We continue to entertain people because that is what makes us feel better. . .because in the entertainment-crazed society in which Americans live, we believe that this is the only way we're going to get people through the turnstiles. Filling the pews and being obsessed with numbers becomes more and more of a priority which, instead of representing God's holy temple, it resembles a sports arena where the clicking of these turnstiles represents the clinking sound of generating cash. As the church grows through man-honoring programs, true unity dissipates. Any idea of honoring the Triune God by being a model of unity through Christ's love has been lost through our homogenized ideology.

Those who have become enamored with the mega-church concept which is spreading across urban and suburban America may take exception to the above assessment. Recently there was a self-assessment study done at one of these churches which counts their attendance in the tens of thousands, to see if the people in their congregation were growing spiritually. The answer was a sobering "no!" They were being entertained and were enjoying the camaraderie/fellowship, but they were not maturing in the faith. I understand the appeal that comes by having a tremendously talented choir and band, resources to build beautiful sanctuaries, Christian schools, and media outreach that includes television, radio, live internet feed, and print capabilities. I also understand how it makes one feel to tell others that you go to "Such and Such, Mega-Mega Church," rather than the 100 person congregation little brick church down the street. Of course, people can more easily hide among the thousands who attend these massive churches and those of color might be able to assimilate into the mass setting more easily than the small town church which is the norm across America, but what are we accomplishing within the commandment of ethnic unity?

Initially, one would think that the Catholic Church would have distinct advantages over evangelical churches in obtaining ethnic unity in their local gatherings since it operates under a parish environment. A parish is a territorial unit which (assumedly) represents the ethnic diversity of that community (if that community is diverse in its make-up), but research gathered by The Polis Center reveals that this is not so. "Catholic parishes represent a different pattern for accepting diversity congregations. While Catholic parishes are proportionally the most diverse compared to other denominations, their diversity results in part from parish boundaries that often cross neighborhood boundaries. Some large suburban parishes encompass several municipalities within one parish. Increasingly though, Catholics choose which parish to belong to, so choice has also become a factor in the diversity of Catholic congregations."[4] In fact, only 5% of black Americans even attend a Roman Catholic Church.[5]

The contemporary church should understand the dynamics between the unity in the true invisible church and the appearance of unity in the local visible church. The true invisible church is comprised of all regenerate people, regardless of the denominational differences, color, or earthly nationality. The local, visible church is comprised of a mixed company of the regenerate and unregenerate (saved and unsaved). Perhaps we need to find our Christian identity more in the eternal body of Christ and less with where we choose to worship. Martyn Lloyd-Jones spoke eloquently of the body:

"The church or body of Christ consists of people of all types and kinds and colors, from many continents and climates. The early Christians are in this body. The martyrs of the Reformation are in this body. The Puritans, the Covenanters, the first Methodists, they are all in this body; and you and I are in this body if we are truly in Christ. The Church spans the continents and the centuries. Natural abilities play no part in this matter. It matters not what you may be, whether you are ignorant or knowledgeable, clever or lacking in faculties, great or small, wealthy or poor. All these things are utter irrelevancies; this body is one. It is the Church of all the ages . . . the fullness of God's people. It is the only body; it is the unseen, mystical church. The one thing that ultimately matters for each one of us is that we belong to this body. We can be members of a visible church and, alas, not be members of this mystical unseen Church."[6]

"RACE CLEAVAGE"

There is a false perception that ethnic division in the contemporary United States has all but disappeared. When you isolate your life from people of color by making (possibly subconscious) decisions that shape your social, work and church life, you begin to create a life which is not representative of the ethnically diverse world that surrounds you. If you really want a reality check, go ask an African American whether the ethnic divide still exists. To use a domestic illustration that all married couples should be able to relate to, husbands have an innate tendency to lie to ourselves about the climate of our marriages. We often think our marriages are doing better than they really are. I often ask men how their relationships with their wives are. The answer is almost universally "pretty good." Then I tell them to ask their wives how well they think their husbands are doing and inevitably, the wives have a less positive impression and assessment of the relationship (me included!). In other words, it doesn't matter what we guys think. It matters what our wives think! The same applies to ethnic relations. Most white evangelicals have deceived themselves into thinking that things between blacks and whites are "pretty good." Really? Go ask an African American what their impression of the relationship is because, it really doesn't matter what whites think. As long as one of the two parties believes the relationship is on life support, it is in critical condition! If we continue to have false impressions, significant changes and healthy relationships will evade us.

Michael O. Emerson and Christian Smith, quoting Brooks and Manza, state that "race cleavage (has) actually grown in magnitude since 1960."[7] These social cleavages are defined by various differences among people which then cause divisions, skin color being by far the largest cleavage. Weren't the turbulent 60s and the human rights movement supposed to eliminate racial tensions and inequality? The church has, sadly, not provided the answers to a world that has searched for a solution for a very long time. Not only hasn't any progress been made within the evangelical church, but true reconciliation has been pathetically sporadic and far too sparse.

One of the major influences that affect how ethnic diversity in a congregation occurs is explained by the previously mentioned Polis Center.

". . .asserting diversity. . . (acknowledges) that these congregations also exist in a diverse social context. For the members, diversity entails a considerable element of tension, with some members eagerly promoting diversity and others resisting it. Yet, as a congregation, they make a vigorous effort to bring the diversity existing around them into their membership. This more aggressive response to a congregation's environment reflects a somewhat different trajectory of congregational and neighborhood change. These congregations reflect a sense of urgency. Sometimes they express a moral commitment — it's what they feel they have to do, or are called to do, despite obstacles. Sometimes denominations require that congregations develop programs for a multi-cultural ministry, although the methods can vary widely. In either case, congregations are pursuing their decision despite internal conflict in its making" (parenthesis mine).[8]

Some Christians are pursuing reconciliation and relationships with Christians who are ethnically different from themselves because they know it is the right thing to do. . .they *must* pursue this because they are compelled to do so. They refuse to take no for an answer because they understand that doing nothing to change the existing culture is wrong. . .it is sinful.

Failure to take action, like taking specific and deliberate steps to create multi-ethnic congregations in our communities, is to allow the existing mono-cultural environment to be the norm. This apathetic approach to doing nothing is reminiscent of what happened to race relations in the U.S. after the Civil War. Within a few short years after the War Between the States, blacks were holding positions of power as U.S. senators, state lieutenant governors, state treasurers, mayors and judges *in the south!* This sudden equality and sharing of power was too threatening to southern whites so Jim Crow Laws were established to separate blacks and whites. This was successful largely because northerners, who had opposed slavery and fought against it, *took a stance of inactivity* and washed their hands of the problem, leaving it to the slavery-supporting south! The north essentially did nothing and, as a result, it would be nearly 100 years before the Civil Rights legislation would be passed. In the previous chapter we mentioned the infamous quote of what happens when good men do nothing. . .case in point! This is the sin of comfort and laziness; the lack of obedience and desire to change into the likeness of Christ.

It was unequal and unloving practices within the post-war church which forced blacks out of the church. The attitude that blacks could worship the same God, in the same church, but not in the same pews and certainly not being allowed to serve as deacons, trustees or elders, is what killed any post-war progress and any hope of multi-ethnic unity. Emerson and Smith state that "almost immediately after the war, before the formal institution of Jim Crow segregation, African Americans in frustration left the white churches en masse to form their own churches."[9] The window of great opportunity to end segregation within the American church closed. . .tightly!

THE EPISTLES ON UNITY

The "Letters" found in the New Testament are chock-full of references to unity that scream for our attention. The early church had their share of prejudice and dissension that led to disunity. In Paul's Letter to the church at Colossae he states that ". . . there is no longer Greek and Jew, circumcised and uncircumcised, barbarian, Scythian, slave and free; but Christ is all and in all" (3:11). The word "barbarian" refers to those who did not speak Greek or had not assimilated into Greek culture. According to the Ryrie Study Bible, "*Scythian* represents the lowest type of uncouth barbarian nomads of southern Russia. In Christ, distinctions of race, class, and culture are transcended."[10] It is difficult for twenty-first century Christians to appreciate the prejudice, disgust, and stigma associated with these dregs of society and yet, Paul is saying to these Christians that they must be practicing unity and love with these fellow believers, and that human distinctions are eliminated by one's union in Christ. God makes no distinctions between humankind, regardless of ethnicity, financial status, skin color, or nationality. All characteristics and genres the world uses to divide and define people become moot. When people are united in Christ the classifications within the church disintegrate. Regardless of what society or individuals may do, we as Christians need to face the issue of ethnic relations within the church and make deliberate and bold decisions to align ourselves with what God requires of us and what He clearly articulates in His Word.

The subject of unity was fresh on Paul's mind as he wrote his letter to the Church at Rome. "May the God who gives endurance and encouragement give you the same attitude of mind toward each other that Christ Jesus had, so that with one mind and one voice you may glorify the God and Father of our Lord Jesus Christ. Accept one another, then, just as Christ accepted you, in order to bring praise to God" (Romans 15: 5-7). Paul prayed that his readers would be given a "spirit of unity" so that they would be able to express this harmonious attitude toward other Christians and, ultimately, glorify God. This is the purpose of Christians, both individually and corporately, to live a life worthy of the calling we have received (Ephesians 4:1; 1 Thessalonians 2:12).

In another of Paul's letters, this one to the church in Philippi, Paul urges us to, "Stand fast in *one* spirit, with *one* mind striving together for the faith of the gospel" (Philippians 1:27). If we indeed share the same body of Christ, we are to stand as one person, not divided. We can love and accept other Christians even when they worship in a different church from across town, but the truth is that even the thought of that scares some believers. Any thought of unity with someone from another denomination shakes them to their very core. I am a big believer that organized religion has done more to turn people away from Christ than to bring them to a saving knowledge of him. Christians do not hesitate to draw the line in the sand when it comes to any suggestion of bridging denominations and compromising on worship style, but the truth is that Scriptural unity is not based on personal preferences. According to Ephesians 4: 13-14, it is "winds of doctrine," that we need to become concerned with because that is what causes division and tosses people in every direction and does not unify. "Winds of doctrine" is "the latest fad or 'teaching' that the popular church latches onto which is full of preferences, personal experiences and questionable interpretations."[11] We should not be ignorant and unaware of false teaching and heresy, but too often it is preferences and interpretations that divide Christians, not biblical truths! So how is true unity achieved? The phrase "in love" is used three times in the above passage. It is love which is the glue that keeps this body of many different and diverse parts together as a harmonious, coordinated and functioning organism. There must also be a common thread of purpose that binds this diversity together; otherwise our cultural differences will pull us apart. The common thread is Jesus Christ, the Savior of all who profess him as the Christ; the Great Mediator between God and man (1 Timothy 2:5).

The Letter of Paul to the Ephesians is a treasure chest of truth, especially chapter 2 where it talks about the importance of unity. Much like the explosive polarizing of whites and blacks in America, the Jews and Gentiles in the early church had deep-seated resentment and animosity towards each other. Paul addresses the problem in chapter 2, verses 14-16 by stating, "For he himself (Christ) is our peace, who has made the two groups one and has destroyed the barrier, the dividing wall of hostility, by setting aside in his flesh the law with its commands and regulations. His purpose was to create in himself *one new humanity* out of the two, thus making peace, and in one body to reconcile both of them to God through the cross, by which he put to death their hostility." The cross has destroyed every barrier for Christians when it comes to unity with all believers around the world.

Albert Barnes, the nineteenth century theologian, makes the following comments on this passage:

> "The Jews regarded the Gentiles with hatred, and the Gentiles the Jews with scorn. Now, says the apostle, they are at peace. They worship the same God. They have the same Saviour. They depend on the same atonement. They have the same hope. They look forward to the same heaven. They belong to the same redeemed family. Reconciliation has not only taken place with God, but with each other. The best way to produce peace between alienated minds is to bring them to the same Saviour. That will do more to silence contentions, and to heal alienations, than any or all other means. Bring men around the same cross; fill them with love to the same Redeemer, and give them the same hope of heaven, and you put a period to alienation and strife. The love of Christ is so absorbing, and the dependence in his blood so entire, that they will lay aside these alienations, and cease their contentions."[12]

Perhaps that was wishful thinking, for in the American Evangelical church, alienation has remained the norm and harmonious peace between blacks and whites is still lacking. Barnes is right, that is *if* Christians act in obedience to Christ and the Holy Spirit. Sadly, American Evangelical Christians seem not very compelled to act on the love of Christ they were so graciously given.

It has been said that ethnic prejudice and the social construct of "race" are learned traits which are easily accepted. I would add that it is nurtured by our sin nature which we all have inherited from our earthy father, Adam. Selfishness manifested through hatred (lack of love is hatred, not indifference) is at the core of this division. Satan divides. Satan, the "great destroyer," has no eternal impact on Christians who have been sealed by the Holy Spirit, but what he can do (and does quite well) is cause division within the body of Christ. He uses the wedge of intolerance, hatred, and jealousy to accomplish his divisive goals. It is a type of war strategy which has been successful for thousands of years, divide and conquer. If, as Barnes suggests, we meet at the base of the cross, that place where our senses are awakened by the too real truth of Christ's sacrifice for the sole purpose of bringing reconciliation between us and God, then the divisive power of Satan is destroyed. The church should be the place where loving, forgiving and accepting actions toward all people is both learned and practiced. Just as the apostle Paul emulated Christ and taught us as much from his actions as from his words, more mature believers have the responsibility to teach newer and younger Christians about the importance of unity.

We simply cannot be content with broken relationships. There is a thought process which all believers need to come to. It is a "heart mentality" which brings wisdom to the mind. It is a conscious decision that makes one realize the need for ethnic reconciliation. Craig Garriott, a pastor of multi-cultural Faith Christian Fellowship located in Baltimore, Maryland describes this passion for reconciliation. "I need this. It is right! I need this for my own sanctification – for my own maturity. I need this because this is the center of the gospel; where God is moving. . .the cross demands it!" And if it is not happening in the community of believers that you associate with, then make it happen!

In that second chapter of Ephesians, (verses 11-22), we find a concentration on the reconciliation of the first century Jews and the Gentiles who, although different in numerous ways, had the most important thing in common, Jesus Christ. Since Jesus destroyed the barrier through his bodily sacrifice and brought peace to all people, unification should not only be a priority, but a pleasure as we move toward being one in Christ. Christ's work on the cross created a new community of people. We should no longer be identified as people of the black community, or people of the white community, or even people of national identity, or this ethnicity or that ethnicity; we have become citizens and heirs of the kingdom of God, the church universal. We are part of God's ethnically diverse family, and part of his holy temple. Jesus' work on the cross "destroyed the barrier," the dividing wall of hostility" so that what was alienation, is now reconciliation, and what was hostility is now peace. In verse 19 we read that "Consequently, you are no longer foreigners and aliens, but fellow citizens with God's people and members of God's household. . ." This household with a Heavenly Father ought not to be dysfunctional.

"Paul's conduct was consistent throughout his ministry and repeatedly the subject of unity was on his heart and mind. He understood the difficulties involving interpersonal relationships between Christians and in Romans chapter 14 we see Paul addressing a group which had diverse backgrounds and upbringings which had tainted their attitudes and practices. There was a serious disagreement among Jews and Gentiles in Rome regarding the issue of what is permissible for Christians (and specifically believing Jews) to eat. The disagreement concerning which foods could and should not be eaten was causing disunity among the broadening family of God. This passage should be seen not so much about dietary laws, as it is about unity amidst differing opinions. Paul preached that harmonious relationships within the family of God were crucial for the health of the church. This applies to the American Evangelical church today as much as it did two-thousand years ago in Rome.

Peter had a similar challenge as described in Acts 10:34-35. "Then Peter began to speak: "I now realize how true it is that God does not show favoritism, but accepts from every nation the one who fears him and does what is right." This was a revolutionary moment of unity for the early church! Peter's words "swept away the prejudice and indoctrination of generations of Judaism."[13] This establishment of the universal church was in its infancy and unity was a fundamental ingredient for its success. In the Book of Acts we see the gospel extended to Samaritans, the Gentiles in Antioch, Cornelius, the Ethiopian eunuch, people of stature and those of modest means, the rich and poor, educated and uneducated. In other words, the gospel was, and is, all-inclusive, does not discriminate against anyone who confesses Jesus as Lord, and it unifies this diversity into a kingdom of priests.

MISREPRESENTING GOD

When we cultivate a mono-ethnic, sub-culture within the church so that true ethnic unity is absent, we misrepresent God and His character and we deceive the world in how we represent God. Instead of representing God as the caring Father whose love compels us to live in harmonious unity with fellow believers, we communicate a lie about who God really is. We are commanded by Jesus to represent God to a lost world, and we can only accomplish that by our loving actions reflected by selflessness. Theologian Max Anders correctly states that "without unity, the world will look at Christians and doubt, based on their relationships, whether Christ is real."[14] True unity reflects Jesus Christ and the diversity of the church and its diversity will bring honor and praise to Jesus Christ as evidence that it is Jesus who unites us. Much of the world is disinterested in Christians and their message because their actions are hypocritical. We preach a message of love, unity and acceptance but practice exclusivity, conformity and "self-sanctioned" and "self-ordained" liturgy. If the Spirit of Christ speaks to our society through the church, then what are we communicating to our society. . .our world?

The local church must be relevant within the community in which it stands and representative of the ethnic and socioeconomic mix around it. We (Christians) are called to be a holy people, consecrated (set apart) for God's good purpose. It is a corporate holiness that the New Testament addresses over and over again, a diversity within unity, which compliments each other in a way which makes the body stronger. Quoting again from Bruce Milne's outstanding book of basic Christian beliefs, "Individual weaknesses, character defects, personality problems, which we all have, are complimented, supported, healed and compensated for by the other members of the body of Christ."[15]

Christian unity among diverse people is a witness of Jesus Christ to the world and a proclamation that he is Savior of the world. Jesus prayed that Christians' love for each other, within their obvious differences in appearance, would be a witness of Him to a lost world. "May they be brought to complete unity to let the world know that you sent me and have loved them even as you have loved me." (John 17:23). The world keeps its eye on Christians and when they see supernatural unity, a true, loving, harmonious togetherness that is seldom seen in our communities, it sees a deep and lasting love that God has for believers and believers for each other. We reflect the nature of God when we are loving, especially to people who appear different than us. The desire for this type of relationship is contagious. The secular world will yearn for what Christians have. The opposite is also true. When we act like a dysfunctional family that exhibits hate, fear and alienation, the world laughs as we make a mockery of the Gospel and Jesus Christ! They look upon the church and Christians and wonder whether Christ is real.

There is a paradox seen in the love-centered message of American Christianity which is not reflected in black-white relations. It is a living contradiction and hypocrisy that has been not only accepted, but subtly nurtured within our churches. One that has its invisible walls not built of brick and mortar, but of policies and programs that express a subliminal message of monoculturalism and that "people who are different from us are not welcome here."

Jesus must be weeping when he looks at the ethnic relations and the lack of unity in the American Evangelical Church today. How sad it must be to him that the secular world has done a better job at ethnic reconciliation than the Christian community. While walking a hospital hallway I recently saw a motivational poster on diversity. The photograph was a beautiful autumn scene with the trees exploding in a multitude of colors. It read:

> The beauties of nature come in all colors
> The strengths of humankind come in many forms.
> Every human being is wonderfully made.
> All of us contribute in different ways.
> When we learn to honor the difference,
> And appreciate the mix, we find harmony.

Why is it that the world which does not love Jesus better understands the goodness of loving their neighbor than professing Christians? Yes, we should be ashamed of ourselves.

Ethnic disunity in the church sends a false message to the world that God is impotent to amalgamate diverse peoples that are already united in spiritual beliefs. In his excellent book, *Jesus and* the *Disinherited*, Howard Thurman asks the inevitable question, "Why is it that Christianity seems impotent to deal radically, and therefore effectively, with the issues of discrimination and injustice on the basis of race, religion and national origin? . . .The question is searching, for the dramatic demonstration of the impotency of Christianity in dealing with the issue is underscored by its apparent inability to cope with it within its own fellowship."[15] We have already been given the Holy Spirit and the resources to beget harmony, but we have lacked the impetus to bring about the long-neglected change that our Heavenly Father so passionately desires. The other day I was listening to Chip Ingram speak on his radio program "Living on the Edge." Although Chip was speaking on marriage, he said something about the need to implement that which you learn in order to bring about change. In other words, ACTION! He said that listening or reading or even agreeing to God's truth does not bring about change. It is only when you put the truth into practice that any change is possible. This is a simple but insightful truth that many Christians ignore. Why? Perhaps because of fear and laziness. Fear of failure and the unknown. Laziness, because it takes effort and time to accomplish change. It's hard work! You may have all the ingredients, but you still have to bake the cake! The flour, eggs, butter, sugar and baking powder do you little good unless you take the initiative to mix them together! What is even more pathetic is that even though Christians have the gift of a Supreme Helper, the Holy Spirit, we fail to call upon this Divine Resource to help us accomplish integrative change.

THWARTING THE WORK
OF THE HOLY SPIRIT

In the Apostle Paul's letter to the church in Ephesus, he paints a picture of who these believers really are in Christ so that they may emulate him and clearly see that they are no longer a part of the lost and sinful world. The New Testament spends much of its time communicating this truth to Christians, because once we see who we really are in Christ, we can more easily live consistently like Christ. When we fail at unity, we fail at experiencing the life that God had intended for us to have. We will lack an important ingredient of the joyful life. Paul tells the Ephesians to "Make every effort to keep the unity of the Spirit through the bond of peace. There is *one* body and *one* Spirit, just as you were called to *one* hope when you were called; *one* Lord, *one* faith, *one* baptism; *one* God and Father of all, who is over all and through all and in all (4:3-6, italics mine). Did you notice how many times the word *one* is mentioned? Seven times the passage emphasizes that there are not numerous or several Triune Gods, body of believers, faiths, hopes and baptisms, but one! Max Anders points out that "since we are unified in this spiritual sense, we should be one in a relational sense. Spiritual unity should be manifested in relational unity."[16] Those of us who have placed our faith and trust in Jesus Christ have been baptized into one Spirit and placed into the body of Christ, as reflected in 1 Corinthians 12:13. "For by one Spirit we were all baptized into *one* body, whether Jews or Greeks, whether slaves or free, and we were all made to drink of *one* Spirit" (NAS, italics mine). In his wonderful commentary on 1 Corinthians, H.D.M. Spence shares, "The diffusion of one spirit is the element of unity. . . Whether we be Jews or Gentiles, whether we be bond or free. Moreover, as these were national and social differences, they were all obliterated by baptism, which made us all equal members of one holy brotherhood (Gal. 3:28)."[17]

When we ignore the prodding and direction of the Holy Spirit we thwart or frustrate his work. How can we frustrate the Holy Spirit? Just before Christ's ascension, Jesus promised to give the disciples (and all believers) an advocate, the Holy Spirit who would be their Helper in the process of becoming transformed into the likeness of Jesus Christ (John 14:16). The term Helper, or Comforter, comes from the Greek "paraclete," the root word suggesting an interceding, strengthening, or advising; things that a good teacher does for a special student. In fact, one of the functions of the Holy Spirit is to teach Christians the truth (John 15:26; 16:13-15). As any teacher will tell you, one of the most frustrating aspects of teaching is when you have a student who thwarts your efforts and ignores your instructions and guidance. This is exactly how Christians frustrate the Holy Spirit, by ignoring the Holy Spirit's prodding and instead, embracing the world. When we fail to act in a way which promotes unity and ignore biblical instruction that teaches us how, we basically disregard the Spirit's work in our lives.

The Apostle Paul in his letter to the church at Ephesus exhorted these fellow Christians to "walk in a manner worthy of the calling with which you have been called, with all humility and gentleness, with patience, showing forbearance to one another in love, being diligent to preserve the unity of the Spirit in the bond of peace" (4:1-3 NAS). This calling not only refers to one's salvation, but also to their responsibility to their union in one body. This responsibility should be manifested in their own personal conduct and toward all believers regardless of their ethnicity. The church is to be a community of unity! Unity is a non-negotiable in the Christian faith. It is not a preference or a choice. We must be reconciled with all our brothers and sisters if we are to reflect the love of Christ and expect to effectively press on in the work of sanctification. When we ignore these instructions found in God's Word we fail to experience the blessings intended for us and fail to utilize the power of the Holy Spirit. As a result, our spiritual growth is stagnant and we continue to walk in disobedience.

The conversion of the Ethiopian eunuch found in Acts 8:26-39 is an excellent example of obedience to God, walking in faith, loving someone who appears different than you, and the positive conclusion that will be experienced. The story begins, "Now an angel of the Lord said to Philip, 'Go south to the road—the desert road—that goes down from Jerusalem to Gaza.' So he started out, and on his way he met an Ethiopian eunuch, an important official in charge of all the treasury of the Kandake (which means "queen of the Ethiopians"). This man had gone to Jerusalem to worship, and on his way home was sitting in his chariot reading the Book of Isaiah the prophet. The Spirit told Philip, "Go to that chariot and stay near it."

Phillip had a choice to make: approach the chariot as commanded or ignore the command and the fellow in the chariot who appeared different than Phillip. The latter would be an example of rejecting the leading of the Holy Spirit. Interesting, the next verse (v. 30) says that Phillip *"ran* up to the chariot" and began a conversation with the man (italics mine). He didn't cautiously walk up to this gentleman, he ran to him! The result was the eunuch's conversion, baptism and his inevitable response of joy!

THE BODY OF CHRIST

The Body of Christ is a figurative concept used by Paul to describe the relationship that believers have to one another, much like how the countless individual parts of the human body work in harmony with each other. It is a spiritual organism which is comprised of all regenerated people from Pentecost (which was the beginning the church, when the Body of Christ was formed by the baptizing work of the Spirit) to the return of Christ. "The relevant and important role that each believer plays within the body should not be overlooked. We need to view ourselves not as individuals detached in an unrelated universe of humanity, but as unique and vital members of a great spiritual body where mutual dependence, respect and necessity is emphasized.

In his book *Breaking through the Boundaries*, the world renowned theologian Henri Nouwen suggested that the celebration of the Lord's Supper is an act which unites the Body of believers. "The Sacrament of the Eucharist. . .has the unique power to unite us into one body, irrespective of age, color, race or gender, emotional condition, economic status, or social background. The Eucharist breaks through all these boundaries and creates the one body of Christ, living in the world as a vibrant sign of unity and community."[19] One of the reasons that the Eucharist is such a unifying sacrament is that when you partake of the body and blood of Christ, you are to confess your sins before your Lord and Savior. You arrive at the cross naked and vulnerable as the beggar we all are and, as a result, have an abstemious mindset. What if black and white churches were to partner with each other and experience this celebration at the Lord's Table together? Could this be a step toward reconciliation? Nouwen continues. "'Jesus prays fervently to his Father, 'May they all be one, just as, Father you are in me and I am in you, so that they also may be in us, so that the world may believe it was you who sent me' (John 17:21). The Eucharist is the sacrament of this divine unity lived out among all people.'"[20]

THE "OTHER" LORD'S PRAYER

The Gospel of John, chapter 17, has been called the "other" Lord's Prayer (vv. 6-19). It is Jesus' prayer of intercession for the apostles and for us, specifically all future believers (vv. 20-26). When you read it, pay attention to how many times you come across the word *one*. I find it interesting that of all the things Jesus could have prayed for and been burdened about when it came to his followers, unity was at the top of the list. Ponder that for a moment. . ..unity! With Jesus' departure from this world the church is now "handed the baton" to continue his work. Of course, this entails spreading the good news of redemption, but Jesus also emphasized unity amongst believers. The Church needs to remember that Jesus' prayer for preservation was a prayer promoting unity of the believers, patterned after the unity of the Trinity (John 17: 21-22). This unity should be of will and purpose. Jesus wanted the diverse peoples of his church to be unified as one, just as he, the Spirit, and the Father are one.

Let me be clear, theses verses are not necessarily calling for an ecumenical movement for establishing a single Christian Church. There are clear and important differences in doctrine between many Christian churches. It is essential that Christians are committed to the revealed truths of the apostolic faith, those truths handed down from the apostles. Milne observes that "It is significant that when Jude intended to write about 'the salvation we share' he found it necessary to urge his readers to 'contend for the faith that was once entrusted to the saints.' (Jude 3)."[21] What Jesus was calling for was cooperation and love among all who have professed their faith and trust in Jesus Christ regardless of color, nationality, or ethnicity. Instead of representing a loving family where we are all brothers and sisters in Christ, we epitomize a dysfunctional family where we ignore each other because of insignificant differences, like ethnicity and the color of our skin!

Jesus' prayer follows his symbolic washing of the disciple's feet. After such a humble act, which again demonstrated that he came to "serve, and not be served" (Matthew 20:28), Jesus prays for our unity. "My prayer is not for them alone. I pray also for those who will believe in me through their (the disciple's) message, that all of them may be one, Father, just as you are in me and I am in you. May they also be in us so that the world may believe that you have sent me. I have given them the glory that you gave me, that they may be one as we are one — I in them and you in me—so that they may be brought to complete unity. Then the world will know that you sent me and have loved them even as you have loved me" (John 17:20-23, parenthesis mine). Jesus was saying that one of our greatest evangelical resources we can bring a lost and hostile world which so desperately needs the life that can only come through Jesus Christ, is to show that we are unified by Christ's love. This unity is modeled by inter-relational love between the Father and Son. Through God's creative diversity among humanity, we are one; we are unified. G.L. Borchert points out that the importance of the significant clause "may they also be in us" (v. 21b), "suggests that the oneness of the community is predicated on a direct relationship of the believers with the Godhead."[22]

The word "love" continues to surface throughout the Gospel of John, as is representative in this seventeenth chapter. Unless we are motivated by love, supernatural love which stems from the "Super-Man," Jesus Christ, true and lasting reconciliation between black and white Christians will remain unobtainable and illusive. Without the power of the Triune God, we are powerless to bring about pure, uncontaminated, reconciliation and genuine love for our African American brothers and sisters and other ethnic Christians as well.

NOTES:

CHAPTER 2: DIVIDED AND CONQUERED
(THE DYSFUNCTIONAL EVANGELICAL FAMILY)

[1]   Martyn Lloyd-Jones, *What is an Evangelical?* (Edinburgh, UK.:The Banner of Truth Trust, 1992), 20-21.

[2]   David K. Lowery, "1 Corinthians," in *The Bible Knowledge Commentary* eds., John F. Walvoord and Roy B. Zuck (Wheaton, IL.: Victor Books, 1983), 508.

[3]   Paul Billheimer. *Love Covers* (Ft. Washington, PA.: CLC Publications, 1981).

[4]   Elfriede Wedam, "Ethno-Racial Diversity Within Religious Congregations in Indianapolis," *Research Notes* vol 2, no 4 (August 1999) [journal on-line]; available from http: http://www.polis.iupui.edu/RUC/Newsletters/Research/vol2no4. htm; accessed 19 Jul 2012.

[5]   The Pew Forum on Religion and Public Life, "A Religious Portrait of African-Americans" [doc. on-line]; available from http://www.pewforum.org/a-religious-portrait-of-african-americans.aspx; accessed 6 May 2012.

[6]   Jones, *What is an Evangelical?*, 59.

[7]   Clem Brooks and Jeff Manza, "Social Cleavages and Political Alignments: U.S. Presidential Elections, 1960 to 1992," *American Sociological Review* 62:937-46 (1997); quoted in Michael O. Emerson and Christian Smith, *Divided by Faith*, (New York: Oxford University Press, 2000), 8.

[8]   Elfriede Wedam, "Ethno-Racial Diversity Within Religious Congregations in Indianapolis," Research Notes vol 2, no 4 (August 1999) [journal on-line]; available from http://www.polis.iupui.edu/RUC/Newsletters/Research/vol2no4. htm; accessed 2 Aug 2012.

[9]   Emerson and Smith, *Divided by Faith*, 39.

[10]   Charles Caldwell Ryrie, *Ryrie Study Bible* (Chicago: Moody, 1995), 1901.

[11]   Tyrone A. Perkins, Pastor of Westside Bible Baptist, interview by author, 28 March 2013, Trenton, NJ, email.

[12]   Barnes' New Testament Notes "Ephesians Chapter 2 Verse 15" [doc. on-line]; available from http://christianbookshelf.org/barnes/barnes_new_testament_notes/ ephesians_-_chapter_2_-_14.htm; accessed 22 May 2012.

[13]   Stanley D. Toussaint, *The Bible Knowledge Commentary, Acts* eds., John F. Walvoord & Roy B. Zuck (Wheaton, Il.: Victor Books, 1985), 381.

[14] M. Anders, "Galatians-Colossians" in *Holman New Testament Commentary Vol. 8:* (Nashville: Broadman & Holman Publishers,1999), 159.

[15] Bruce Milne, *Knowing the Truth*, 265.

[16] Howard Thurman, *Jesus and the Disinherited* (Boston: Beacon Press, 1976), xix.

[17] Ibid.

[18] H. D. M. Spence-Jones, ed., *1 Corinthians. The Pulpit Commentary* (New York: Funk & Wagnalls, 1909), 399.

[19] Site de prière et de meditation, " Breaking Through the Boundaries" [doc. on-line]; available from http://meditations.be/Breaking-Through-the-Boudaries; accessed 14 Jul 2012.

[20] Ibid

[21] Milne, *Know the Truth*, 290.

[22] G.L. Borchert, The New American Commentary, John 12–21 (Nashville, Broadman & Holman Publishers, 2002)., Vol. 25B: (NAC).

3

THE SECOND GREATEST COMMANDMENT

Owe no one anything, except to love each other, for the one who loves another has fulfilled the law. Romans 13:8

For you were called to freedom, brothers. Only do not use your freedom as an opportunity for the flesh, but through love serve one another. Galatians 5:13

Beloved, let us love one another, for love is from God, and whoever loves has been born of God and knows God. 1 John 4:7

*I*t seems as though contemporary Christians have focused on the greatest commandment, to "love the Lord your God with all your heart and with all your soul and with all your mind,"[1] at the expense of ignoring the second greatest commandment, "Love your neighbor as yourself.'[2] Jesus' answer to the teacher of the Law went beyond the immediate and intended question of which commandment is the most important (as if obeying the most important one would give us brownie points if we disobey others) by stating that the commandment to love God is inseparable from the commandment to love others. "Teacher, which is the greatest commandment in the Law? Jesus replied: 'Love the Lord your God with all your heart and with all your soul and with all your mind. This is the first and greatest commandment. And the second is like it: Love your neighbor as yourself. All the Law and the Prophets hang on these two commandments'" (Matthew 22:36-40).

How is it that all of the commandments can be summed-up in these two commands? Each of the Ten Commandments can be described as either a vertical command, that which is directed toward God, or a horizontal command, that which is directed toward people. By listing the Ten Commandments below, we can easily see the direction of each command.

1. "You shall have no other gods before me." Vertical.
2. "You shall not make for yourself an idol in the form of anything in heaven above or on the earth beneath or in the waters below, or any likeness of anything that is in heaven

65

above, or that is in the earth beneath, or that is in the water under the earth. . ." In other words, don't create any idols for yourself. It should be noted that God defines an idol as anything which you love more than God. Anything that stands between the two of you. Vertical.

3. "You shall not misuse the name of the LORD your God. . ." Vertical.
4. "Remember the Sabbath day by keeping it holy." Vertical.
5. "Honor your father and your mother. . ." Horizontal.
6. "You shall not murder." Horizontal.
7. "You shall not commit adultery." Horizontal.
8. "You shall not steal." Horizontal.
9. "You shall not give false testimony against your neighbor." Horizontal.
10. "You shall not covet your neighbor's house. You shall not covet your neighbor's wife. . ." Horizontal.

The first four commandments are vertical commands, commands requiring covenant obedience to God, who is to be above all other relationships. The following 6 commandments are horizontal commands, commands regarding how we are to treat other human beings. Jesus' comments on the "two great commandments" of Deuteronomy 6:5 ("Love the Lord your God with all your heart and with all your soul and with all your strength") and Leviticus 19:18 (". . .love your neighbor as yourself. . .") incorporate the entire Ten Commandments. If I love God with my entire being I will not love any other more than him; create idols, use His name in vain, or disrespect the Lord's Day. By the same token, if I love other human beings at least as much as I love myself (in other words, if I am truly selfless), I will respect my parents, I will not murder or commit adultery. I will not steal, lie about what I saw, or desire possessions that other people have. The commandments that Jesus classified as "the greatest" are so comprehensive that they cover any and all of the 601 laws (commands) found in the Old Testament. These two commands are joined together so that if you fail at one, you will fail at the other. I cannot love God if I do not love people (who are created in God's image)! It is impossible! If we do not love people because of the color of their skin or their ethnicity, I do not love God! Jesus was so radical that he took the second greatest commandment to, what most Christians find to be, an absurd level! He said, "You have heard that it was said, 'Love your neighbor and hate your enemy.' But I tell you, love your enemies and pray for those who persecute you" (Matthew 5:43-44). Love my enemies? Love an Islamic Extremist? A terrorist? Apparently, yes. Jesus made no distinction as to whom we can choose to love and whom we do not. He made a carte blanche statement, and meant what he said. Love everyone!

The truth is that *most* Christians have a problem loving their neighbor. But who is my neighbor? Jesus offers an extensive and comprehensive definition of who are neighbor is by including not only "everyone" we come in contact with, but specifying the command to love our enemies as well (that covers just about everyone). Howard Thurman adds, "Once the neighbor is defined, then one's moral obligation is clear. In a memorable story Jesus defined the neighbor by telling of the Good Samaritan. With sure artistry and great power he depicted what happens when a man responds directly to human need across the barriers of class, race, and condition. Every man is potentially every other man's neighbor. Neighborliness is nonspatial; it is qualitative. A man must love his neighbor directly, clearly, permitting no barriers between."[3]

Obviously, one can look at the word "neighbor" and expect that to mean those who live nearby, and in many cases that means people who look like me, act like me, are of the same socioeconomic status as me. . .people who are "easy" to love (what is almost funny is that most of us have difficulty loving even those people similar to ourselves!). Perhaps the phrase "Fellow Citizen" might be a bit more appropriate. "Fellow Citizen" suggests a common bond. Answers.com defines it as "a person who is from one's own country: compatriot, countryman, countrywoman." Paul spoke of our reconciliation with our Heavenly Father through Christ's atoning work which unites in the family of God. "Consequently, you are no longer foreigners and aliens, but *fellow citizens* with God's people and members of God's household (Ephesians 2:19, emphasis mine).

Throughout history, Christians have demonstrated God's love in tangible ways by meeting people's physical and material needs.

Christians have changed the world in immeasurable ways including building hospitals and schools, providing clean drinking water in desolate areas and responding to the basic needs of people suffering from natural disasters like famine, earthquakes and floods. Until the world sees how much Christians care about people, they will never want what (or more specifically, whom) we have. The commandment to love others, seen as a horizontal act, always points vertically to Jesus Christ. Giving selflessly of one's time, effort, money and self, is the essence and power of the second greatest commandment. Supernatural love from above is a love which is expressed without obligation or expectation of repayment or reciprocation. It is the only resource which can penetrate deep-seated indifference and prejudice.

We all have felt rejected at one time or another. For most of us, it is the worst of all experiences and yet, when given the opportunity to befriend a stranger, we often reject them. Oh, maybe not directly. It may not be obvious to those around us, but the fact remains, we snub them. That is the quandary in which we find ourselves. We do that which we don't want done to us. The "do unto others" quote popularized by the phrase "The Golden Rule" was never spoken by Jesus, at least not verbatim, but his teaching clearly accentuated the moral behind the phrase. It was an important part of the Ten Commandments. "Love your neighbor as yourself: I am the LORD."(Leviticus 19:18).

Actions speak louder than words. You see, love is not a feeling, it is an action, and in that vein, a choice. "Feelings" are fleeting. . .they change as the wind changes from one direction to another. Infatuation is perhaps the most wonderful feeling in the world. The adrenalin and high we *feel* is like none other, but time normally quiets the overpowering emotion and a sense of clarity (and often reality) surfaces. Faults and weaknesses of the person whom your love is directed towards become much more evident as the infatuation wanes. If love was nothing more than a feeling, few of us would ever remain in love with someone. Infatuation is often born of selfish motives stemming from the self-centered perspective of "I like what I am getting from this person. I love how I feel when I'm with this person. I like what this person does for "me." There are a lot of "me's" and "I's" involved in infatuation. The list of those benefits we receive from this person is lengthy, but includes self-worth, confidence, sex, a sense of belonging, a lack of loneliness and ego-stroking. All selfish desires.

Love is nothing more than selfish smoke and mirrors unless it is an unforced expression, visible by action, which puts the recipient of the love before the giver. God demonstrated his love for us through Jesus Christ and gave us eternal life. Our actions also need to be sacrificial. John tells us, "Dear friend, you are faithful in what you are doing for the brothers and sisters, even though they are strangers to you. They have told the church about your love. Please send them on their way in a manner that honors God. It was for the sake of the Name that they went out, receiving no help from the pagans. We ought therefore to show hospitality to such people so that we may work together for the truth" (3 John 1:5-8). What are those of us in white churches doing to help those black churches who are hindered by the lack of resources? Here are fellow brothers and sisters who have "gone out" for the sake of Jesus Christ, to make converts to the faith and disciples of our Lord and Savior. This is an investment worth our time and money! Nothing less than our loving generosity would be 'honoring to God' who demonstrated his love for us by giving us his Son.

It is because God loved us, with unconditional, sacrificial love, that we love him. It is *only* in our love that we can serve, honor and obey him. Without the motivation of love, serving God will be a burdensome chore. That is why so many people drift from the faith. They are trying to serve Christ in their own power, which is limited, weak and feeble. The commitment and loving relationship we have with God, our Father, is a covenant relationship. Bruce Milne explains well that the Triune God expresses an "inter-trinitarian" love amongst the Three Persons. He explains it this way:

- "the Father is love: 'God so loved the world that he gave his one and only Son,' writes John (John 3:16);
- The Son is love: 'the Son of God, who loved me and gave himself for me,' cries out Paul (Gal. 2:20);

• The Spirit is love: 'I urge you by the love of the Spirit,' says Paul again (Rom. 15:30).

The word here, *agape*, has comparatively little currency beyond the N.T. The common Greek term, *eros*, speaks of a love which relates to a *worthy* object, while *agape* is a love for the unworthy, for one who has forfeited all right to the lover's devotion."[4]

This explanation brings Romans 5:8 into better focus. "But God demonstrates his own love for us in this: While we were still sinners, Christ died for us." While we were God's enemies, while we hated God, He expressed *agape* love for us, the unworthy. Do we subconsciously decide who is worthy of our love and who is not? Jesus didn't and neither should we. If we are undeserving of God's love and yet receive it free of charge, who are we not to pass it on to all peoples.

1 JOHN – AN EXHORTATION TO LOVE

Everything a Christian needs to know about loving their fellow believers can be found in the Book of 1 John. In chapter 2, John uses darkness and light to illustrate that before we were reconciled to God, we were in the dark; a confused state, but now, through Jesus Christ, we have been illuminated in our understanding of God's revelation which is hidden to nonbelievers. "Dear friends, I am not writing you a new command but an old one, which you have had since the beginning. This old command is the message you have heard. Yet I am writing you a new command; its truth is seen in him and in you, because the darkness is passing and the true light is already shining" (vv.7-8). Is John saying that this command was old or new? This was not a new command; on the surface there is nothing new here, it is a reiteration of the second greatest commandment. John is elaborating on God's commands and so this is a review of what his readers would have already known. Yet, this command is new; it had not lost its fragrance like a new bloom. The command to love was first manifested by Christ by his self-sacrificing life and death and then by his followers motivated by a new and eternal life offered through the grace of God.

John continues to lay out his argument concerning how essential love is. "Anyone who claims to be in the light but hates a brother or sister is still in the darkness. Anyone who loves their brother and sister lives in the light, and there is nothing in them to make them stumble. But anyone who hates a brother or sister is in the darkness and walks around in the darkness. They do not know where they are going, because the darkness has blinded them" (vv. 9-11). Ouch! What's there not to understand? If you don't love your brother or sister, that fellow-heir of God's heavenly kingdom, you're lost! You are stumbling around in the dark! The kingdom of God is characterized by light and love. John's comments are reminiscent of Jesus' teaching found in the "Sermon on the Mount," where Jesus says ""Let your light shine before men in such a way that they may see your good works, and glorify your Father who is in heaven" (Matthew 5: 16). God's Son is telling us that our faith should be a light in a world made dark by sin and that it should manifest itself in good deeds motivated by love. John was warning his readers against a very present danger and was affirming that a Christian who hates his brother must question whether he has, in fact, been transformed from the darkness into the light. This truth is repeated in the third chapter where John reiterates that "Anyone who hates another brother or sister is really a murderer at heart. And you know that murderers don't have eternal life within them" (1 John 3:15 NLT). At the very least, such a person cannot profess to have an intimate relationship with Christ and, at best, remains an infant in the faith (Ephesians 4: 11-15; 1 Peter 2:1-3).

1 John 4:7-21 clearly describes both God's love for us and how it should be manifested on earth by our love for others. This passage begins: "Dear friends, let us love one another, for love comes from God. Everyone who loves has been born of God and knows God. Whoever does not love does not know God, because God is love" (vv. 7-8). This is pretty plain and simple! The Christian who does not truly love fellow believers has no idea who God is. How can you be a Christian, an adopted son or daughter of the Heavenly Father and not know who your Father is? Just as we all bear some physical resemblance to our earthly fathers, so too we all should have a spiritual resemblance to our Heavenly Father. We understand

the necessity to love because we are God's children. We learned it from our Father (1 John 3:10-24) by watching Him, just as children we watched and learned from our earthly fathers. Love for others, regardless of the differences we may have, is evidence that one is a child of God. As his children, we are to love others, especially fellow believers, just as God exemplified his love for us. "We love because he first loved us. Whoever claims to love God yet hates a brother or sister is a liar. For whoever does not love their brother and sister, whom they have seen, cannot love God, whom they have not seen. And he has given us this command: Anyone who loves God must also love their brother and sister" (1 John 4: 19-21). Clearly, it is impossible to love God if we do not love our brothers and sisters. It is simply inconsistent with the truth and if we profess love for God and yet hate other believers, we are liars about our affection for God. Strong words.

"This is how God showed his love among us: He sent his one and only Son into the world that we might live through him. This is love: not that we loved God, but that he loved us and sent his Son as an atoning sacrifice for our sins. Dear friends, since God so loved us, we also ought to love one another (vv. 9-11). This love was initiated by God, not by man. God's love, demonstrated through Christ's atoning sacrifice, is the model by which every Christian should extend their love for others. God and Christ are leading us by their examples. Verse 12 is the key verse; the verse that defines the entire chapter. "No one has ever seen God. But if we love each other, God lives in us, and his love is brought to full expression in us" (NLT). How else is a lost world ever to see God? The invisible God is made visible when God's love is experienced among Christians. As stated earlier, when we are not demonstrating love and unity to a world lost without Christ, we misrepresent the character of God. Love needs to be expressed to *all* people, even strangers, as we represent Jesus Christ in the microcosm of the world that God has placed us in. This love should be, at the very least, conveyed in nonverbal, visible actions toward others. In the multi-ethnic, multi-cultural environment of Christ's worldwide church, our obvious expression of love towards each other will be seen by others and through us, they will see Christ. D.L. Akin artfully explains this verse.

"Indeed, we are incapable as finite sinful creatures of looking on God. It would certainly be our death. He can be seen, however, in the lives of those who demonstrate his love to others. . .The second section of the verse opens with a third-class conditional sentence ("if we love one another") which leaves the possibility of not fulfilling the condition. Unfortunately, not everyone who professes to be a child of God manifests this kind of mutual love. But it is God's rightful expectation since it is the demonstration that God who revealed himself in Christ is also revealed in the lives of those in whom he "abides" (translated "lives"). In fact, this mutual love is the evidence that this has taken place. A person loves because God has come to dwell within him. This is how the love of God is brought to its goal. . .The love one has for other believers will demonstrate the fact that one is indwelt by God. The source for this kind of love is a personal and permanent union between God and the believer secured at the cross of Calvary."[5]

Psychologist Gordon Allport's Scale of Prejudice is a measure of the manifestation of prejudice in a society. It includes: Antilocution, Avoidance, Discrimination, Physical Attack and Extermination.[6] It is a progressive and cancerous escalation of hatred and prejudice which is gradual by nature. Antilocution is when a majority group freely makes jokes about a minority group, often including negative stereotypes and "hate" speech. Allport's scale may be dismissed by the evangelical community as irrelevant to their lack of ethnic integration, but the alienation, lack of interaction, and the avoidance of one's neighbor due to color tells another story of nonfiction. In his now famous book, "The Nature of Prejudice" (1954), Allport defined prejudice as "thinking negatively of others without sufficient justification."[7] As a follower of Christ, we are to never look down on another person regardless whether the world thinks we have justification to do so or not. Allport said that "It is easier—and probably cheaper—to smash an atom than a prejudice."[8] This human impossibility is exactly why only the church must take the lead on reconciliation. Allport's quote, of course, fails to consider the supernatural work of the Holy Spirit and how people continue to be completely transformed into new spiritual beings.

Children of God love each other. When they experience God's love for them they are astonished because nothing in this world can compare; it is alien in nature and its magnitude is truly incomprehensible. The NIV misses the mark in translating 1 John 3:1a, by excluding the imperative "see" or "behold." "How great is the love the Father has lavished on us, that we should be called children of God! And that is what we are!" The NASB translation reads "See how great a love the Father has bestowed on us, that we would be called children of God; and such we are." The imperative draws our attention and demands contemplation of the extent of God's amazing love toward his children. As Hiebert states: "This love, originating with God, ever seeks the true welfare of those being loved; it is amazing indeed when we remember the personal destitution of those He loves. God is a love that works visible, transforming results in the lives of its recipients."[9]

Visible, transforming results. Anything less should be considered suspect. An attitude of deliberate ignorance and obliviousness threatens our universal witness to a lost world. If we cannot love our neighbor, how can we offer God's love to those who are lost? The answer, of course, is that we cannot. Our perception of our calling has been warped by the sins of selfishness and comfort. We manipulate the gospel into that which makes us comfortable. What we do is create our own form of Christianity where we get to choose and reject biblical mandates so that our "religion" is one that comes easy to us. We try to appease God and the aching conviction brought on by the Holy Spirit. Our misconception is that the Great Commission does not apply to us because we are not called to be missionaries or pastors. We conveniently become oblivious to the fact that, if we have been redeemed by Christ and adopted by God, we are modern-day disciples. Jesus never intended it to be that narrowly defined. Christ was speaking to us as much as he was the eleven on the day of ascension when he communicated our need to share the blessings that we have received. Are we so deceived that we believe we can choose whom we will love and whom we will not? It is impossible to express social love without having regard for the rights of others.

Before we can share the gospel with someone, we need to *earn* the right to do so. That means loving that person in tangible ways and to possess a burden for them that without a personal relationship with Jesus Christ they are going to hell. That means loving them enough to risk rejection, reputation, and position. The all-inclusive way we have been called to love is the best sermon someone could ever preach. Your verbal message comes when an observer of your life asks why you have such joy, peace, love and purpose. "But in your hearts set apart Christ as Lord. Always be prepared to give an answer to everyone who asks you to give the reason for the hope that you have. But do this with gentleness and respect. . ." (1 Peter 3:15). When you treat all people with respect, dignity and Christ's love, it will be seen by others as extraordinary. As Christians, we are in the business of building bridges. I guess you could call us "Spiritual Civil Engineers." Our training is not from a university but from God's Word and our mentor, the Holy Spirit.

WITHOUT SUPERNATURAL HELP, TRUE LOVE IS IMPOSSIBLE

There is no doubt that loving others is impossible to achieve in our own power and strength. Let's be honest, some people are very hard to *like*, let alone love, but that is exactly why we must be empowered by the Holy Spirit and compelled by Christ's love for us in order to be obedient to this command. I've never heard a sermon fully explaining the characteristics and work of the Holy Spirit, and so it's no wonder that so many Christians remain ignorant of their greatest ally, helper and friend here on earth! It is amazing how very rarely we Christians *call* upon the Holy Spirit. . .how seldom we *pray* to Him. By giving the Holy Spirit, Jesus empowered his disciples, not only those who followed him during his ministry here on earth, but all those for future generations. This was part of Father's infinitely wise plan, knowing that when Jesus returned home to heaven we believers would be left all alone to fight for ourselves, wandering around life trying to find our way home. The Holy Spirit teaches us (John 16:12-15), guides us (Romans 8:14), gives us assurance (Romans 8:16) and intercedes for us in prayer (Romans 8:26; Ephesians 6:18). All Christians have been "born-again" (John 3:1-8; 2 Corinthians 5: 17; 1 Peter 1:2) and as a result, have the indwelling of the Holy Spirit (John 7:37-39; Acts 2:38; 2 Thessalonians 2:13). Why then wouldn't we call upon He who is best qualified to help us through the ongoing process of sanctification? The Holy Spirit can and *will* empower us to love others as we yield to His teaching and directing of our lives. Our love for others, especially those who appear "different" than us, should be conspicuous and openly exhibited through our actions. Not by polished acting but by a genuine expression of the grace we have received from our Heavenly Father through Jesus Christ.

Our actions need to be visible works, or "good deeds," which include standing for justice, especially for those who do not have a voice; the fringe of society, the poor. "Love does not delight in evil but rejoices with the truth. It always protects. . ." (1 Corinthians 13: 6-7a). Our love should extend to *all people* as if we were associated by consanguinity, for fellow believers *are* our spiritual brothers and sisters whom we share more important characteristics with than our biological family. This desire and passion for unity is so alien to the world that they will be drawn to this supernatural love empowered from above. It is the most powerful witness to a lost and desperate world. Bruce Milne describes the origin of this love within the context of fellowship. "Fellowship (Gk. Koinonia) and the church's glorifying God are closely linked: 'Accept one another, then, just as Christ accepted you, in order to bring praise to God (Rom. 15:7). As Christians live together in true fellowship, God is magnified. . .our love for one another within the community of faith needs to take its normative pattern from God's love for us displayed for all time in the self-sacrifice of Jesus: 'Love each other as I have loved you' (John 15:12). Love of this quality is not a human possibility, which is why the NT consistently speaks of it as a gift of the Holy Spirit (Rom. 5:5)."[10]

It should be noted that love does not come easily or naturally to men as it does to women. Other than Titus 2:4, the scriptures do not emphasize that women are to love their husbands, perhaps because God knew they wouldn't have much difficulty doing that. He commanded them to *respect* their husbands (Ephesians 5:33; 1 Peter 3:1), something all men long for. Men, on the other hand, are consistently commanded to love their wives (Ephesians 5:25, 28-29, 33; Colossians 3:19). Women find their self-worth through relationships, and so love is more easily developed and extended to others. Men, on the other hand, get their self-worth from work. I am convinced this is why women outlive men. When most men retire, they lose their sense of purpose and identity. They lose the respect found in accomplishing tasks and a job well-done. When women retire, they find themselves with more free time enabling them to do more of what they love, spending time with family and friends. . .relationships. Perhaps this is why the Bible consistently reminds us of how, why and whom we are to love. The entire Bible has an underlined theme of love as we see commands to love and explanations on how to love throughout both the Old and New Testaments.

Let's see what God has to say about love by looking at some verses on the subject:

"My command is this: Love each other as I have loved you."

John 15:12

"We love because he first loved us."

1 John 4:19

"And now these three remain: faith, hope and love. But the greatest of these is love."

1 Corinthians 13:13

"And you are to love those who are foreigners, for you your-selves were foreigners in Egypt.'

Deuteronomy 10:19

"The foreigner residing among you must be treated as your native-born. Love them as yourself, for you were foreigners in Egypt. I am the Lord your God."

Leviticus 19:34

"Love does no harm to a neighbor. Therefore love is the fulfill-ment of the law."

Romans 13:10

"Keep on loving one another as brothers and sisters."

Hebrews 13: 1

"You, my brothers and sisters, were called to be free. But do not use your freedom to indulge the flesh; rather, serve one another humbly in love."

Galatians 5:13

"Be completely humble and gentle; be patient, bearing with one another in love."

Ephesians 4:2

"Now that you have purified yourselves by obeying the truth so that you have sincere love for each other, love one another deeply, from the heart."

1 Peter 1:22

"Dear friends, let us love one another, for love comes from God. Everyone who loves has been born of God and knows God."

1 John 4:7

These are earnest appeals and a constant reminder for Christians to love others, and not only those whom we already have a relationship with, but to those who are currently strangers to us. There is an assumption in these verses that the one who is in God, will love like God loves. . .that it is a natural expression since we are our Father's children. Do not miss the fact that there is a close relationship between those who are humble and selfless and those who love. That should make perfect sense to us because the definition of love is to put the welfare and needs of others before your own. The problem is that most American Christians have difficulty loving their neighbor. Not, of course, those people who we share similarities with, or who come from the "right" side (our side) of the tracks, but those who appear different than ourselves. A large part of the problem lies in our pride and lack of humility. All and any sense of pride must be suffocated so that the fresh air of humility can be breathed in.

Do you think that our love for other Christians is important to God? Listen to what David wrote in Psalm133:1-3. "How good and pleasant it is when God's people live together in unity! It is like precious oil poured on the head, running down on the beard, running down on Aaron's beard, down on the collar of his robe. It is as if the dew of Hermon were falling on Mount Zion. For there the Lord bestows his blessing, even life forevermore." The Bible Knowledge Commentary explains the relevance of the oil that consecrated the high priest, Aaron. "This imagery from the priesthood was appropriate because of the pilgrims being in Jerusalem. The oil poured on Aaron's head flowed down on his beard and shoulders, and onto the breastplate with the names of all 12 tribes. The oil thus symbolized the unity of the nation in worship under the consecrated priest. As the oil consecrated Aaron, so the unity of the worshippers in Jerusalem would consecrate the nation under God."[11]

WHO IS THE WORST OF ALL SINNERS?

In a secret sense, we all tend to judge people on whether or not they are deserving of our love. Those who do us harm, physically, emotionally, economically, in regards to our reputation or stature and position in society, are normally judged as undeserving of our love, and the secular world would and does quickly agree with us. Of course, we reject people based on other criteria, like financial status, education, or even whether they are obese or have a different skin color or accent. We excuse our actions by lying to ourselves (and others) that it isn't that we do not love them, we simply have such great differences that we would rather not associate with them, after all, we have nothing in common, right? Interestingly, if God loved only those who are worthy of his love none of us would experience his grace and acceptance.

I would like to suggest an approach to re-educate the way will look and receive others. . .all others. In 1 Timothy 1:15 Paul makes a bold, but honest (from his perspective) statement. He says, "Here is a trustworthy saying that deserves full acceptance: Christ Jesus came into the world to save sinners—*of whom I am the worst*" (emphasis mine). Paul honestly believed he was the worst of all sinners because he looked inwardly instead of outwardly, where comparisons are created. He first took a long, hard look at his own sin and his total depravity and understood his unworthiness as he stood before God. This heart-humble attitude gave him a fresh perspective on everyone he met. If *he* is the worst sinner, than logically speaking, everyone else is better than him. Everyone he meets is *deserving* of his love and acceptance because he is not better than them. It wasn't until I embraced this truth that I could begin loving people in a genuine way. No one is beneath deserving my love and acceptance, no matter who they are or what they have done. It wasn't until then that I took on 1 Corinthians 15:10 as my life verse, loosely translated, "I now understand that my sordid past was simply a backdrop on which to display (God's grace) the grace of God."

For many years I had great difficulty loving others, especially those who were different than me (which, if the truth be known, was just about everyone!). One day, I read (again) the Apostle Paul's statement that he was the worst of all sinners (1 Timothy 1:15). I thought, "Man, Paul was worse than me? No way!" Of course it dawned on me that Paul lived 2000 years before I had entered the scene. Had Paul been my contemporary perhaps he would have said, "I am the second worst sinner in the world!" There is a true humility present when you take a sobering and truthful look at your own depravity. Paul exhorts his readers to have this same type of humility and selflessness: "Do nothing out of selfish ambition or vain conceit. Rather, in humility value others above yourselves, not looking to your own interests but each of you to the interests of the others" (Philippians 2:3-4). Until you understand your own depravity you will always have difficulty loving those who you currently view as inferior to you. When your broken and contrite heart (Psalm 51:17) mourns over your total and complete sinfulness, only then will you begin to look at others as better than yourself, and when that happens there is no reason *not* to love anyone else.

Where does one begin to delve into that which stirs fear and painful memories, to call those memories from that distant place they were exiled to, hoping never to be seen or heard of again? The true understanding of one's own depravity is a horrible, dirty experience, which is probably why so few Christians dare go there, but the risk is worth the experience and the reward, for it will produce a beautiful appreciation for God and others. In the quiet of the day, when you are not distracted by the noise of the world, meditate on the inclinations of your heart. Be honest and stop allowing yourself to lie about how "good" you are. Stop comparing yourself to others for "who among men knows the thoughts of a man except the man's spirit within him? In the same way no one knows the thoughts of God except the Spirit of God" (1 Corinthians 2:11). What is it that God requires of you and me? Above all else, God requires a broken and contrite heart (Psalm 51:17), my friend, and that will escape you until you grasp your own depravity. When you come to this place where you are not intoxicated by pride, you realize that you *are* the worst of all sinners and the grace of God becomes very real to you. When you have arrived at this beautiful place you can view *all others* as better than yourself and worthy of love, kindness, forbearance and gentleness fueled by joy, peace, self-control and faithfulness (Galatians 5:22-23). One of the marks of a true Christian is that they will love God's people. Do you love God's people? All of them?

I often find it helpful to read some of the early church fathers or works by the seventeenth century Puritan writers. The perspective is one free from the distraction and temptation of affluence and comfort, which provides and unadulterated approach to self-humility and graciousness. A book that was especially helpful to me was St. John of the Cross' poem and treatise entitled *Dark Night of the Soul,* which describes the journey to purification of the soul. The "darkness" represents the pain and extreme privation the soul faces in detachment from the world as it reaches the ecstasy that comes from union with its Creator. The Christian life is not a passive, painless journey of indulgence and having all your wishes come true. On the contrary, if done correctly, it is a life of self-abandonment and surrender of all that is dear to you. Jesus taught this premise when he said, "If anyone comes to me and does not hate his father and mother, his wife and children, his brothers and sisters--yes, even his own life--he cannot be my disciple" (Luke 14:26). Quite obviously, Jesus was not asking his followers to literally hate their parents. What he was saying was that nothing or no one should come before one's devotion and dedication to Christ. Period! It was a testimony to the difficulty that comes with discipleship. That is why there are many more "pretenders" in the Christian faith than there are committed disciples, giving evidence to the fact that "The door to heaven is narrow" (Luke 13:24).

Dark Night of the Soul was written while John of the Cross was imprisoned by his Carmelite brothers for attempting to reform the religious Order, a goal shared by his friend, Teresa of Avilla. The text also describes the ten steps on the ladder of mystical love derived from Saint Thomas Aquinas' writing. I found that it was only in the realization of the depths of my sin and depravity that I could gain true perspective of God's grace through Jesus Christ. I understood that it is only in losing ourselves that we can ever find ourselves (Matthew 10:39). This is not really as paradoxical as it may sound. Many of us have been deceived into believing that we are "better" than we really are. We're "okay," certainly when compared with others. It is exactly this prideful comparison mentality which warps our Christian perspective and our calling to love others. It is the exact same sinful blindness that Jesus criticized the Pharisees for their prideful condemnation of others. "As he taught, Jesus said, 'Watch out for the teachers of the law. They like to walk around in flowing robes and be greeted in the marketplaces, and have the most important seats in the synagogues and the places of honor at banquets'" (Mark 12: 38-39). The long flowing robe was a sign of wealth and position.

Jesus again taught about the danger of trusting in yourself and viewing others with contempt when he told the Parable of the Prayers of the Pharisee and the Tax Collector (Luke 18:9-14). The Pharisee's prayer was centered on telling God how good of a person he was by using his obedience to the Law, fasting, and tithing as evidence and comparing himself to others as his measuring stick. The tax collector, on the other hand, used God as his measuring stick for his righteousness and so he easily saw his unworthiness and need for God's mercy and forgiveness. Jesus used this story to illustrate the prerequisite of humility before God in order to receive forgiveness and that those who remain proud will be brought low by God.

When we can reach a point of humbleness (not an artificial facade, which actually is a form of pride; the "woe is me" syndrome, but rather a killing of "self"), we begin to view people in a very different light, much more like Jesus did. People become valuable as we acknowledge their worth and see them as being worthy of our love; then a desire for unity blossoms. People's visible (and invisible) differences are seen as something to appreciate and celebrate rather than something that divides us. A lack of love is inevitable when you look down on people, but by placing yourself on the bottom rung of the ladder, you are constantly looking up at others.

WHAT DOES LOVE REQUIRE?

When we accept Christ as our Lord and Savior nothing should ever be the same. Our response to this loving and unlikely adoption should be to reflect the characteristics of our new (and eternal) Father. The question a Christian should ask in regards to ethnic relations is "How can we express to others the love we have received from Christ?" As stated earlier, this love needs to be motivated by selflessness in a manner which places the needs of others ahead of one's own; a sacrificial love, much like that of Christ's love for us. Without this selfless approach, we are in danger of falling into the trap of paternalism simply to appease our conscience. Paternalism is an attitude that demonstrates "superficial good deeds" for another person from a position of authority and superiority, much like how a father shows pity upon a child. This kind of expression of love creates a dependency upon the "father" image instead of a true helping hand so that the individual can become independent. This is the error in our government's handling of welfare. Instead of temporary assistance to help the poor meet physical and material needs coupled with education and training so that they are empowered to be self-sufficient, our state and federal governments have created a society dependent upon the government while they remain powerless and eternally poor. Paternalism is a condescending attitude toward helping the "little people" rather than a loving approach of lending a hand to another brother or sister in need.

A selfish offering to your brother would be to give used clothing that is faded, soiled, torn or stained. A loving offering would be to purchase new clothing and give it with the brand and instruction tags still on the garment. A selfish offering would be to layer a thick coat of paint on the rotted and decayed wood of an African American church. A loving offering would be to team up with black brothers and sisters and help finance the building of a new, beautiful sanctuary. A selfish offering would be to offer those canned goods to the food pantry which are past the expiration date or those items you don't like to eat anyway. A loving offering would be to purchase the top shelf goods that are in need and desired by the impoverished. It would do us well to remember why God rejected Cain's sacrifice (Genesis 4:3-7). Cain's brother, Abel, gave the firstlings of his flock, the fat portion was considered to be the richest part of the animal, and so Abel brought his best, reflecting his desire to please God. Cain, on the other hand, carried out his act of worship more as an obligation, simply an attempt to fulfill his duty and be done with it. One offering was selfish and the other selfless. You cannot appease God. Are you a Cain or an Abel?

Love requires more than a willingness for change; it requires the mobilization of one's self in taking an active role in reconciliation. That requires an attitude that "if I don't do something about this problem, no one will." It is the refusal to pass the buck and assume that someone else will solve the problem, or that it simply isn't your problem to worry about. It is my problem. It is your problem. It is our problem.

For the black community, love requires the ability to honestly forgive white brothers and sisters for both their prejudice as well as their forefathers' sinful actions. We all must remember that this is an obligation required of all who seek God's mercy (Matthew 6:12). Forgiveness from the black community, liberates the white community *and sets us free to pursue reconciliation*. Henri Nouwen hits the nail on the head when he states, "To forgive another person from the heart is an act of liberation. We set that person free from the negative bonds that exist between us. We say, "I no longer hold your offense against you." But there is more. We also free ourselves from the burden of being the "offended one." As long as we do not forgive those who have wounded us, we carry them with us or, worse, pull them as a heavy load. The great temptation is to cling in anger to our enemies and then define ourselves as being offended and wounded by them. Forgiveness, therefore, liberates not only the other but also ourselves. It is the way to the freedom of the children of God."[12] Refusing to forgive your white repentant brother will result in a bitterness of spirit stirred on by Satan and an impotent ministry (2 Corinthians 2:9-11). "Get rid of all bitterness, rage, and anger, brawling and slander, along with every form of malice. Be kind and compassionate to one another, forgiving each other, just as in Christ God forgave you" (Ephesians 4:31-32). Fellowship with God is impossible if one refuses to forgive their fellow brother or sister in Christ. Regardless of whether or not our black brothers and sisters forgive us, the white community must do the right thing and act in obedience to God's commands. God extends love to us, even when we refuse it. While we were still God's *enemy*, God loved you and me enough to send his Son to die for us (Romans 5:8); therefore, we must love, regardless of whether it is reciprocated.

The First Epistle of John exhorts believers to live a life of obedience to God while loving their Christian brothers and sisters. In his commentary of this book, Zane Hodges states that Christians who have experienced God's love, demonstrated in Jesus Christ, should be able to see the manifestation of this through the love Christians have for each other (1 John 4:14). "This great truth can be put on display through the instrumentality of Christian love."[13] This can only be realized through righteousness and Christlike love. In Paul's Letter to the Romans, he states, "For it is not those who hear the law who are righteous in God's sight, but it is those who obey the law who will be declared righteous" (2:13). It is with boldness that Christian's are to do God's bidding in the world, for what else is there but to be obedient to God while living in a world which is increasingly godless? The church is a type of "outpost" placed in the wild, wild world that is at enmity with God. When we think of an outpost, we think of the American frontier, and the similarities are worth noting. Hine and Faragher, describe the frontier history as ". . .a tale of conquest, but also one of survival, persistence, and the merging of peoples and cultures that gave birth and continuing life to America."[14] The difference is that we Christians *do* possess a Manifest destiny! Through the Great Commission, we have been instructed to make disciples and called to a great "expansion," across all nations (this "Manifest Destiny," however, is a bit different from what the 19th century Americans had in mind when looking for justification to expand across the North American continent!).

Loving reconciliation will take boldness from both the white and the black church and a passion for biblical unity regardless of the cost. It requires looking at the brother within your own church who opposes action towards reconciliation and lovingly admonishing him. We need to be committed to expressing our love in real, tangible ways, not because the civil rights legislation decreed it, not because we want to prevent a racial revolution or violence, not because it is politically correct, but because we are compelled to by Christ's love for us (2 Corinthians 5:14). This love from Christ should stimulate deliberate reciprocal action in us, manifested by loving others. It is the mystery of reconciliation between God and us through Christ which compels us to love others. "So from now on we regard no one from a worldly point of view. . .all of this is from God, who reconciled us to himself through Christ and gave us the ministry of reconciliation: that God was reconciling the world to himself in Christ. . .And he has committed to us the message of reconciliation. We are therefore Christ's ambassadors, as though God were making his appeal through us" (2 Corinthians 5: 16a, 18-19a, 19c-20a). Once Paul became a believer in Jesus Christ, he no longer evaluated people based on external appearances. This is all done with the heart's desire and motivation to bring people to a saving knowledge of Jesus Christ. Showing indifference toward others who are different than you is a damaging testimony to the world.

One of the themes of the New Testament is love, seen throughout John's gospel, as fulfillment of the Law (Romans 13:8), as the two greatest commands (Matthew 22:36-40), and as the "revelation of the character of God that is to be reflected in relationships within the community of believers (1 John 4:7-8),"[15] which is the church. The twenty-first century church, however, has not always been faithful to these truths, commands and characteristics. Instead of being the salt or light to a world lost without Christ, we have shunned what we know to be right and promoted a divisive religion that places a dark veil upon the hearts of non-believers so that they turn from the truth of the gospel. One of the reasons for the decline of interest in Jesus

Christ and Christianity in the West is what the world observes in our treatment of fellow brothers and sisters.

Love and a desire for unity should come as naturally to the spiritually transformed body as breathing does. It should be a spiritual motor response, like exhaling, where it dissipates upon the atmosphere of human existence. A natural product of this love would be the desire and need for fellowship with brothers and sisters in the faith. Every gathering of Christians, regardless of one's nationality or ethnicity, should be a spiritual family reunion worthy of celebrating with love and kindness. Fellowship has always been part of God's design for man. Even before the fall, God demonstrated that fellowship was necessary for man by declaring that "loneliness" was not good (Genesis 2:18). As humans were made in God's image, we see this same emphasis placed on fellowship with the Three Persons of the Trinity. The story of the New Testament is one of God's plan of redemption for lost humankind and their response within the community of believers. Milne reminds us that "Cain's question, 'Am I my brother's keeper?' (Genesis 4:9), receives an emphatic 'yes' from Scripture. We are not alone, nor were we ever intended to be; we were made through and with and for our human neighbor."[16] We remain defiantly incomplete when we ignore the need for, and fail to take action towards, developing racial reconciliation.

If we truly want to become transformed into people who love all people, we must look to Him who loved the world so much that he died for it. The Son of Man came to serve and reconcile the world to God, his Father, through the power of love. Christ's entire life exemplified this love for others, especially those who were on the fringe of society. "Follow God's example, therefore, as dearly loved children and walk in the way of love, just as Christ loved us and gave himself up for us as a fragrant offering and sacrifice to God" (Ephesians 5:1-2).

For those of you who have consistently loved others with a Christlike love, please do not lose faith, but continue to set an example to those who appear weaker in the faith. Your love will have a contagious effect and it is servants like you from which lasting change will come. "Now about your love for one another we do not need to write to you, for you yourselves have been taught by

God to love each other. And in fact, you do love all of God's family throughout Macedonia. Yet we urge you, brothers and sisters, to do so more and more. . ." 1 Thessalonians 4: 9-10.

NOTES:

CHAPTER 3: THE SECOND GREATEST COMMANDMENT

[1]   Matthew 22:36-37.

[2]   Matthew 22:38.

[3]   Howard Thurman, *Jesus and the Disinherited* (Boston: Beacon Press, 1976), 79.

[4]   Milne, *Knowing the Truth*, 92.

[5]   D.L. Akin, *1, 2, 3 John* in *The New American Commentary* (30) Vol. 38: (electronic ed.). Logos Library System (Nashville: Broadman & Holman Publishers, 2001).

[6]   WPH, "Prejudice and Allport Scale" [doc. on-line]; available from http://www.wphomes.org.uk/about-us/Equality_and_Diversity.aspx; accessed 6 July 2012.

[7]   Gordon W. Allport, *The Nature of Prejudice* (Cambridge, Mass.: Addison-Wesley Publishing Company, 1954), 537.

[8]   Psychoanalytic Electronic Publishing, "The Nature of Prejudice" [doc. on-line]; available from http://www.pep-web.org/document.php?id=paq.023.0605a; accessed 18 Aug 2012.

[9]   D.E. Hiebert, "The Epistles of John" (1991): 138; quoted by D. L. Akin, D., *1, 2, 3 John. The New American Commentary* (Nashville: Broadman & Holman Publishers, 2008), 282.

[10]   Milne, *Knowing the Truth*, 300.

[11]   Allen P. Ross, "Psalms," *The Bible Knowledge Commentary OT*, eds., John F. Walvoord and Roy B. Zuck (Wheaton, Il.: Victor Books, 1983), p. 888.

[12]   Nouwen, *Bread for the Journey*, January 26.

[13]   Zane C. Hodges, *The Bible Knowledge Commentary NT*, eds., John F. Walvoord and Roy B. Zuck (Wheaton, Il.: Victor Books, 1983), 899.

[14]   Robert V. Hine and John Mack Faragher, *The American West: A New Interpretive History* (New Haven, CT.:Yale University Press, 2000), 10.

[15]   Richard B. Hays, *The Moral Vision of the New Testament* (New York, HarperOne, 1996) , 200.

[16]   Milne, *Knowing the Truth*, 131.

4

CHRIST-LIKE MEANS "LIKE" CHRIST

Follow my example, as I follow the example of Christ.
1 Corinthians 11:1

Carry each other's burdens,
and in this way you will fulfill the law of Christ.
Galatians 6:2

In your relationships with one another, have the same
mindset as Christ Jesus.
Philippians 2:5

*7*he New Testament calls Christians to respond faithfully to God's calling as individuals, but more importantly as the church, to a shared life of discipleship. When we respond faithfully to such a calling we experience an authentic Christian community reflective of Christ's love. It is only in our attempt to model our lives after our Eternal Superhero that we can achieve anything that resembles righteous living and unity within a diverse gathering of people, commonly called "the church." It is to Christ we look for answers on how to live our lives in a way that is pleasing to our Heavenly Father. I look to Christ in order to understand how to love my wife, and the Apostle Paul tells me to love her *sacrificially*, "just as Christ loved the church and gave himself up for her" (Ephesians 5:25). When I am struggling with any relationship, odds are I have taken my eyes off of Jesus. Whether it is reacting to people's comments and actions, or simply how to treat people, I must not only look to Jesus' commands (Mark 12:31), I must look at Jesus' *life*.

How did Jesus treat people? We can look at his interaction with anyone he came in contact with, but his encounter with the man who had leprosy (Mark 1: 40-45) provides an excellent example for us. In that society, a leper was considered to be both physically unclean (since it is contagious) and ceremoniously unclean (Leviticus 12-15; Numbers 5:2), but Jesus reached out and *touched* the leper to heal him.[1] Certainly, the Son of God could have simply said the word and the man would have been healed. But Jesus looked upon the leper as one worthy of his time and ministry, not only to address the man's physical needs, but his emotional and spiritual needs as well. A man who was rejected by society, was loved and accepted by the ultimate King. This was quite evident when Jesus met the Samaritan woman at the well (John 4: 1-26). This is another paradigm of how Christ treated people, especially those viewed as unworthy of conversation, one's time, and most of all, love. He looked upon the woman's heart and saw her need for "living water."

Jesus was a man of action (thank God!). In Mark's gospel we see the author emphasizing more on what Jesus did than what he said. His empathy for people did not remain as an emotional response, one absent from tangible acts; rather he backs up his words with works. Over and over again we see that (first) Jesus was moved with compassion when he saw the suffering of people, and (second), his compassion resulted in taking action to elevate that suffering. Jesus did not look at people, have pity and compassion for them, and then walk away. Why should we? Perhaps it was more through Jesus' actions than his words that these people were drawn to him for he addressed their physical needs before pursuing their spiritual needs. So too, we must address people's physical needs in order to earn the right to address their spiritual needs. The old cliché rings true: people don't care how much you know until they know how much you care. I am reminded of a poem I read many years ago:

Your Holiness and My Loneliness

I was hungry and you held meetings to discuss my hunger.
I was imprisoned and you crept off quietly to pray for my release.
I was persecuted and you explained to me how Christ was persecuted.
I was sick and you knelt down and thanked God for your health.
I was homeless and you preached to me of the spiritual shelter of the love of God.
I was lonely and you left me alone to pray for me.
You seem so holy and I'm still very lonely.

Author Unknown

There is no better way to begin building bridges between diverse peoples than to reach across the divide to form friendships and help meet their material needs. That is a tangible way of expressing Christ's love. After all, that's what families do.

The goal of the Christian life is to emulate Jesus Christ as we draw on the sanctifying power of the Holy Spirit. Our focus is two-fold; both internally for our own spiritual family by developing disciple-making disciples, and externally by sharing the Good News of Jesus Christ with those who are lost. Neither of those goals is possible if we do not emulate our Lord and Savior. If imitation is the sincerest form of flattery, then Christians ought to imitate Jesus, not to flatter him, but to honor, respect, and glorify him through obedience. The best teachers have always been those who lead and teach by example. They not only paint a picture of how the task should be done, but they demonstrate the technique, often in the most difficult circumstances from which their students can learn. Christians are to be life-long apprentices of Christ as they express what they have learned in the pragmatic arena of life. We are to imitate our Master as we observe his actions and reactions through detailed eyewitness testimony found in the Gospels. The Apostle Paul helps us connect the dots between Christ's actions and our proper response as he instructs various churches throughout the Near East. Replicating Christ's actions plays an important role in fostering a Christian's process of sanctification, the transformation into the likeness of Christ. Paul said to "Follow my example, as I follow the example of Christ" (1 Corinthians 11:1). Paul lived his life that way, always with his eyes up, fixed on the cross. As Jesus humbled himself in obedience, even to death (Philippians 2:6-8), Paul suffered in his obedience to Christ (2 Corinthians 11:23-27; 12:10). When the community of God lives in obedience to God's Word, the result will always be a grace-filled representation of Christ and his love for others.

Christians should understand that in order to become like Christ we are to patiently unite our suffering with His. "For just as we share abundantly in the sufferings of Christ, so also our comfort abounds through Christ. If we are distressed, it is for your comfort and salvation; if we are comforted, it is for your comfort, which produces in you patient endurance of the same sufferings we suffer.

And our hope for you is firm, because we know that just as you share in our sufferings, so also you share in our comfort" 2 Corinthians 1:5-7. There is a sense here that unpleasant circumstances for the name of Christ will be accompanied by an overwhelming comfort. This concept (and truth) is alien to most Americans who have been manipulated and deceived by the god of affluence and comfort. It is in those places around the world where persecution and poverty are the norm that the church is growing, both in numbers and in spiritual development. People who have next to nothing monetarily are sharing in their poverty because they understand what it is to be Christlike. They understand sacrificial giving and both the church and individuals outside the church are being richly blessed.

Within this suffering, Jesus understood what it was like to be discriminated against due to ones' ethnicity and social status. Jesus lived in a place and time when Jews lived under the oppression of Roman power. He was disenfranchised by society, not because he was the Son of God, but because he was a poor Jew, which in this ancient culture meant you were inevitably marginalized. Howard Thurman brings clarity to this important fact by pointing to the dedication of Jesus as an infant:

"There is recorded in Luke the account of the dedication of Jesus at the temple: 'And when the days of purification according to the law of Moses were accomplished, they brought him. . .to the Lord; (as it is written in the law of the Lord, Every male that openeth the womb shall be called holy to the Lord;) and to offer a sacrifice according to that which is said in the law of the Lord, A pair of turtledoves, or two young pigeons.' When we examine the regulation in Leviticus, an interesting fact is revealed: 'And when the days of her purifying are fulfilled, for a son,. . .she shall bring a lamb of the first year for a burnt offering, and a young pigeon, or a turtledove, for a sin offering. . .And if she be not able to bring a lamb, then she shall bring two turtles, or two young pigeons; the one for a burnt offering and the other for a sin offering.' It is clear from the text that the mother of Jesus was one whose means were not sufficient for a lamb, and who was compelled, therefore, to use doves or young pigeons.

The economic predicament with which he was identified in birth placed him initially with the great mass of men on the earth. The masses of the people are poor. If we dare take the position that in Jesus there was at work some radical destiny, it would be safe to say that in his poverty he was more truly Son of man than he would have been if the incident of family or birth had made him a rich son of Israel."[2]

To be born in a stable is not the beginning for one of high social status. Jesus' understanding and empathy for those who live on the fringe of society was an experience realized within his fully human side. Howard makes a parallel between the suffering of blacks under white dominant rule and that of Jews under Roman rule. ". . .Jesus was a member of a minority group in the midst of a larger dominant and controlling group."[3]

Relationships cause some of the largest challenges and stresses in our lives. When we look in God's Word for answers to these relational problems we first need to observe Christ's interaction with others, even those who culturally were much different than he was. Christ's love for people consistently broke down every barrier that society created. Our reading and study of the Scriptures must result in obedience and implementation of the truths we learn. "But if anyone obeys his word, God's love is truly made complete in him. This is how we know we are in him. Whoever claims to live in him must walk as Jesus did" (1 John 2:5-6). Smalley concludes: "The summation of the moral law of God is to be found in the command to love; and this love is exemplified supremely in the life and ministry of Jesus, whom believers are called to imitate."[4] Obedience to God's Word (which is his command) results in a complete and full relationship with God and His love. The reverse is also true. "Whoever says, 'I know him,' but does not do what he commands is a liar, and the truth is not in that person" (v.4). So it's only reasonable to deduce that the person who says they have a relationship with God, but does not *love* his fellow Christian who has a different skin color, "is a liar, and the truth is not in that person." We see this again with even stronger language in 1 John 3:10; "This is how we know who the children of God are and who the children of the devil are: Anyone who does not do what is right is not a child of God; *nor is anyone who does not love his brother*" (emphasis mine). There is a clear understanding here that both children of God and children of the devil can be identified by their actions. This truth should not be missed or overlooked.

Does this imply that such a person will not experience God's saving grace? I think a distinction needs to be made between habitual sinning with no desire to turn from that way of life, and those who have been born a second time and given the divine nature of God. The latter is one who, although not perfect or sinless, hates their sin, confesses and turns from it. The former is one who practices sin and shuns biblical instruction (1 John 2:19). Zane Hodges explains; "Heresy in the Christian church, whether on the part of its saved members or unsaved people in it, always unmasks a fundamental disharmony with the spirit and doctrine of the apostles. A man in touch with God will submit to apostolic instruction (cf. 1 John 4:6)."[5]

If we look at the fourteenth chapter of John's Gospel, we see that an obedient disciple experiences a special kind and level of love from the Triune God. "Whoever has my commands and keeps them is the one who loves me. The one who loves me will be loved by my Father, and I too will love them and show myself to them. . . Jesus replied, "Anyone who loves me will obey my teaching. My Father will love them, and we will come to them and make our home with them" (John 14: 21, 23). The true test of love is obedience. There is a reward for loving the Father that is not given to those who are disobedient. Jesus and His Father will manifest themselves to the Christian who demonstrates their love for them by the Father loving them and the Son revealing Himself and, as a result, there's a veracity of abiding with the believer, and the believer abiding with the Triune God. It is a special and unique relationship.

The ability to love others in an unselfish and Christlike way can only be achieved when we are empowered by God Himself through the Spirit. This obedience is possible when we abide in Christ and submit to the Spirit. Jesus taught us that the only way to achieve the characteristics that are seen in him is to be grafted into Christ.[6] He said, "Remain in me, as I also remain in you. No branch can bear fruit by itself; it must remain in the vine. Neither can you bear fruit unless you remain in me. I am the vine; you are the branches. If you remain in me and I in you, you will bear much fruit; apart from me you can do nothing" (John 15:5). It is impossible for the branch to bear fruit separate from the Vine. Gerald Borchert explains that this is an elementary truth of discipleship, to remain in Christ, for "a branch is not a self-contained entity, and neither is the Christian disciple. And as a branch separated from the supply of nourishment cannot produce fruit, neither can the Christian. Fruit bearing for the disciple is totally dependent on a direct connection with Jesus. Attachment to Jesus or abiding in him is, therefore, the sine quo non (an indispensable action or ingredient) of Christian discipleship"[7] (parenthesis mine). The natural progression of this thought is seen a few verses later (v.6) when Jesus states that a branch that produces nothing is worthless and when it dries up should be thrown into the fire and burned. The assumption is that true disciples of Christ *will* bear fruit because they *will* remain in Christ. If what Jesus said is true, that those who remain in the Vine (Christ) will naturally bear fruit, then why is deliberate segregation within the church the norm? The Apostle Peter gives us the answer to that question in one of the most dramatic scenes in the entire Bible.

In Matthew chapter 14, it is not Jesus' walk on water that astonishes me, It is that Peter is able to do it too! Blomberg brings a perspective to this passage which is often overlooked. "Peter asks for the power to imitate Jesus' miracle. 'If it is you,' (v.28) is a potentially misleading translation for a first-class condition. The logic more closely resembles that of 10:1, 8, when Jesus passes his miracle –working authority on to his disciples. *Since it is you, please enable me to do the same thing you are doing* better captures the intent of Peter's request."[8] Jesus grants Peter's request and Peter walks on the water toward Jesus, but before he reaches Jesus, Peter begins to doubt, resulting in his immediate sinking where he cries for help. Blomberg continues: "The word "doubt" (from Greek *distazo*) suggests the idea of trying to go in two different directions at once or of serving two different masters simultaneously. Having lost his initial faith, Peter is unable to go on, begins to sink, and is rescued. His cry echoes the plea of all the disciples in 8:25. Jesus rebukes Peter for wavering, as he did all the disciples in 8:25. . .the real significance and focus of this scene is that it rests more with Peter's failure than with his accomplishments."[9]

With his eyes fixed on Jesus, Peter could do *anything,* including walking on water, but the instant he looked away, he began to tread water! As we *remain* in the Vine (Christ Jesus) we can have confidence, not only of our eternal future, but that we will be transformed into the likeness of him and will be empowered to accomplish great things! Our ability to love others as Christ loved us does not and cannot come from our strength and ability. "Through these he has given us his very great and precious promises, so that through them you may *participate in the divine nature*, having escaped the corruption in the world caused by evil desires. For this very reason, make every effort to add to your faith goodness; and to goodness, knowledge; and to knowledge, self-control; and to self-control, perseverance; and to perseverance, godliness; and to godliness, *mutual affection; and to mutual affection, love. For if you possess these qualities in increasing measure, they will keep you from being ineffective and unproductive* in your knowledge of our Lord Jesus Christ" (2 Peter 1:4-8, emphasis mine). These gifts are extremely valuable and effective and give us the enabling power to participate in God's nature. We become like Christ!

In order to have an ever-increasing resemblance to Christ, it only makes sense that we must spend personal time with him. . .alone! There is great benefit to group fellowship, Bible study, and corporate worship, but your greatest growth in intimacy with Christ will come as you spend more one-on-one time with Him. In Mark 3:14 we are told that Jesus selected the 12 disciples so that they might spend time with him (and learn from him). They became "guilty by association" (even to death) and became known as "little Christs," (originally a derogatory term given to believers at Antioch, Acts 11:26). As we obey the words of Jesus, our relationship with him deepens, and we have an increasing hunger for his communication to us through reading God's Word, prayer, and meditation.

One of my pet peeves is that many Christians are still distracted by the worries of this world and have been deceived into chasing after fleeting "vapors" that promise joy and fulfillment. They forget about their first love, Jesus, who is more than able to satisfy all our desires, and so, these people produce little fruit and are stunted spiritually. Some of these believers are the same people Jesus was referring to when he told the parable of the sower and the seed (Matthew 13:1-23). "The seed falling among the thorns refers to someone who hears the word, but the worries of this life and the deceitfulness of wealth choke the word, making it unfruitful" (v. 22). Those with little faith harvest little. Jesus uses a parable for the first time in Matthew's Gospel and explained to his disciples that the "mysteries of the kingdom of heaven" were given to them so that they might understand the meaning of the parable. Jesus' followers have been given certain privileges that others have not. Those of us who have placed our faith and trust in Jesus Christ possess this discerning knowledge as we lean not on our own understanding but on his divine wisdom. God's revelation through the Scriptures is one way he makes himself known, and while God's Word makes sense to us, it is nothing but foolishness to non-believers (1 Corinthians 1:18).

Jesus quotes the prophet Isaiah in this parable to remind his disciples that his edict of the word will result in the spiritual senses of those who are self-righteous and calloused to become dull. The word callous refers to something that was once soft but has become hard. Like the rocky soil, those who refuse to repent and change produce little to no fruit in their lives. When opportunities arrive to make Christ-honoring decisions which may cost that person something (time, effort, prestige, money), there is no response. They heard the message of Jesus Christ with joy, but like the rocky soil, they did not let it take root in their lives. They received the gospel intellectually, but didn't let it take root in their heart so that the Holy Spirit could produce an effectual faith, a faith which produces spiritual growth and manifests itself in capitalizing on opportunities to expand the kingdom of God.

In chapter 7 of Matthew (verses 15-23 and Luke 6:43-44; 13:25-27), Jesus speaks about true and false prophets and disciples. These are people who pretend to be followers of Jesus Christ, but in reality are frauds. He then goes on to say that a bad tree produces bad fruit and a good tree, good fruit. Perhaps not very profound, but it raises an obvious and simple question. Are you producing good fruit? In regards to the subject of ethnic reconciliation within the church, something you know God is passionate about, what condition is your fruit in? Is it juicy, full and ripe, or rotten and worthless? God doesn't want superficial Christians. He doesn't need them. God knows the heart of people and the motives of their heart. Christ condemns the Laodicean church and its pastor in Revelation chapter 3 for their half-hearted commitment. "I know your deeds, that you are neither cold nor hot. I wish you were either one or the other! So, because you are lukewarm—neither hot nor cold—I am about to spit (literally, vomit) you out of my mouth" (Revelation 3: 15-16, parenthesis mine).

We are all given opportunities that will help mold our spiritual formation. We must look for these opportunities and welcome them for what they are intended to do. . .transform us into the likeness of Christ. We are being transformed from one degree of glory to another as we observe the glory of Christ (2 Corinthians 3:18). Jesus taught that the goal and purpose of any student is to be like the teacher. "The student is not above the teacher, but everyone who is fully trained will be like their teacher" (Luke 6:40). When we have become a "new creation" in Christ through faith and trust in Him, we "have put on the new self, which is being renewed in knowledge in the image of its Creator" (Colossian 3:10; Romans 8:29).

THE HUMILITY OF CHRIST

What many of us lack in our attempt to emulate Christ is a humility that places others before ourselves. It is selfishness which stands between us and reconciliation with other believers. Unity and sacrificial love not only suffers, but is virtually impossible without a humble heart. Imitating Christ is not a choice or a preference for Christians; it is an obligation and necessity of the Christian life. Jesus was the epitome of humility demonstrated by the fact that the Son of the Living God came to earth with the mission of a true servant; to serve, not to be served (Matthew 20:28; Mark 10:45). All that he accomplished on earth was with the motivation and desire to minister to others and bring glory to his Father. His command to love others and to work towards unity stemmed from the love and unity that the Father, Son, and Spirit shared.

The reason for Jesus' command to be the salt and light of the world is twofold. The first is because we are to hunger for righteousness. We are to set ourselves apart (not physically, but spiritually) from the world and reflect Christ in all that we do! It is our responsibility to be holy, just as God is holy (Leviticus 11:44; 1 Peter 1:16). The second, and the context in which Jesus was using these illustrations, is so that Christ can be seen in us by the world. The invisible God is thus visible through the loving actions we exhibit. When we fail to reach out to those who are ethnically different than us and genuinely love them, we are failing to see the personal worth of those who are also made in God's image.

Again, if we have any hope of becoming Christians who love others and openly stand against injustice and ethnic discrimination, then we must make obtaining humility a never-ending quest. It requires the daily surrender of self and the commitment to transfix one's eyes upon Jesus. Paul's exhortation to humility, in Philippians chapter 2, is for believers to share the same heart attitude that the Son of God had. The passage begins: "Therefore if you have any encouragement from being united with Christ, if any comfort from his love, if any common sharing in the Spirit, if any tenderness and compassion, then make my joy complete by being like-minded, having the same love, being one in spirit and of one mind" (vv. 1-2). Spiritual unity is the result of God's love in believer's hearts. It is in this groundwork that Paul rests his plea for believers to be Christlike which has a prerequisite of having the humility of a servant. When Christians will rely on the power of Christ, this unity is possible.

"In your relationships with one another, have the same mindset as Christ Jesus: Who, being in very nature God, did not consider equality with God something to be used to his own advantage; rather, he made himself nothing by taking the very nature of a servant, being made in human likeness. And being found in appearance as a man, he *humbled* himself by becoming obedient to death — even death on a cross!" (Philippians 2: 5-8, emphasis mine). The phrase "made himself nothing" has also been translated "emptied himself" (NAS) and is also called the *kenosis*. There has been some debate and mis-understanding regarding what exactly Christ emptied himself of. It's safe to say that Christ was completely God and fully man, a paradox that will always be difficult for us to grasp. It may be better to look at this phrase as an incredible act of humility whereas the Son of God surrendered his heavenly position, dignity, and preincarnate glory in order that he might become the perfect sacrifice for our sins. He emptied himself of those things he deserved as the Second Person of the Holy Trinity. It is Christ's condescension that, though he was rich, he became poor (2 Corinthians 8:9), and he did that for people like you and me who were completely out of options for being reconciled to God the Father. Christ could have called a legion of angels to rescue him from the cross, but instead he suffered torture and a brutal death in order that we might have life (Philippians 2:7; Isaiah 53). The chorus of the hymn written and composed by Roy Overholt simply captures this incredible truth:

> He could have called ten thousand angels
> To destroy the world and set Him free.
> He could have called ten thousand angels,
> But He died alone, for you and me.

Any hope of reconciliation between two parties must begin with repentance and humility. The beauty of humble repentance is that it tears down barriers. It is an acknowledgement that I have sinned against you, I am mournful over that sin, and I would like you to forgive me (not so that my guilty conscience can be repaired, but so that a healthy relationship can either begin or be restored back to health). It is where pain and hope meet; where we forgive just as we have been forgiven. As Reverend Garriott (FCF) states, "Christ has already reconciled us. That is a fact! It is our responsibility to celebrate that and apply it!" We need reconciliation with God. We need reconciliation with *all* of God's children. Henri Nouwen eloquently writes that reconciliation with our neighbor is dependent upon us realizing and enjoying our reconciliation with Christ:

Claiming Our Reconciliation

"How do we work for reconciliation? First and foremost (it is) by claiming for ourselves that God through Christ has reconciled us to God. It is not enough to believe this with our heads. We have to let the truth of this reconciliation permeate every part of our beings. As long as we are not fully and thoroughly convinced that we have been reconciled with God, that we are forgiven, that we have received new hearts, new spirits, new eyes to see, and new ears to hear, we continue to create divisions among people because we expect from them a healing power they do not possess.

Only when we fully trust that we belong to God and can find in our relationship with God all that we need for our minds, hearts, and souls can we be truly free in this world and be ministers of reconciliation. This is not easy; we readily fall back into self-doubt and self-rejection. We need to be constantly reminded through God's Word, the sacraments, and the love of our neighbors that we are indeed reconciled.[10]

Nouwen reminds us that humility is more than a mindset (which, if you are anything like me, the mind can be too easily distracted); it is a "heartset." It is love in the purest sense of the word, where one puts others ahead of themselves. It is self-less-ness. The apostle Peter challenged Christians to "Show proper respect to everyone: Love the brotherhood of believers, fear God, honor the king" (1 Peter 2:17). More literally, "Honor everyone." Why? Simply because each human being has been uniquely created in God's image. That is reason enough. The insertion of the command to "fear God," is not a reference to be afraid of our Heavenly Father in nervous terror. Jesus' reconciling work on the cross has given Christians the access to our Father's throne by which we can boldly enter into His presence (Mark 15:38; Hebrews 10:21-22; Ephesians 3:12). Rather, that reverence and awe toward God leads to obedience. As we stated in the previous chapter, one must love and honor others if they hope to love and honor God, and one cannot truly love and honor God without loving and respecting all of his human creation. The two are inseparable and yet many Christians have failed to comprehend this elementary truth. H.H. Hobbs offers three simple rules that form the basis for ethnic harmony.

1. All persons have a common origin: God.
2. All persons have a common need: God.
3. All persons have a common purpose: God.[11]

True humility coupled with transforming faith is contagious. People all around us are lost and seeking this type of faith and it is this reconciling humility and harmony which is a more powerful witness than any words. But first we must get right with God. The Psalmist had the right idea:

> "Create in me a pure heart, O God,
> and renew a steadfast spirit within me.
> Do not cast me from your presence
> or take your Holy Spirit from me.
> Restore to me the joy of your salvation
> and grant me a willing spirit, to sustain me.
> Then I will teach transgressors your ways,
> so that sinners will turn back to you.
> You do not delight in sacrifice, or I would bring it;
> you do not take pleasure in burnt offerings.
> My sacrifice, O God, is a broken spirit;
> a broken and contrite heart
> you, God, will not despise.

Psalm 51: 10-17

SERVNG THE POWERLESS

Jesus never hung out with the "in" crowd. Many of us would rather associate with the more popular, or successful, or intellectual than we would those who seem to have less to offer because, in our selfishness, we tend to seek relationships that benefit us. We quickly take our eyes off of Jesus and his perfect example and instead, drown in the attitudes that we adopt in order to fill our self-serving needs.

The first century church at Corinth also forgot that Christ was supposed to be the focus of their faith; that Jesus was their example and that their transformation into his likeness was to be their quest. Like many contemporary Christians in the affluent West, the Corinthians thought they had arrived. Their egotistical arrogance had them believing that they were better than everyone else because they enjoyed prosperity and were given special spiritual gifts. It was the first "name it and claim it" theology that is so prevalent today (also referred to as the "blab it and grab it" or "prosperity theology"). It is the false teaching and belief that God's will is for all Christians to be blessed with good health and financial prosperity (will God

106

bless all Christians? Yes, but not necessarily financially and physically). This is supposed to be accomplished through donations to Christian ministries, positive thought, personal empowerment, and faith. These are the exact same deceiving tactics that Satan used in the garden with Adam and Eve; the promise that "you will be like God" (Genesis 3:5b). And so the Corinthians thought they were superior to everyone else, looking down on those who had fewer earthly treasures or less spectacular spiritual gifts.

In his letters to the Corinthians, Paul addressed Christian's disregard for the poor and the various fractured relationships within the church. This lack of concern for fellow believers was also evident in the way the poor were mistreated in celebrating the Lord's Supper. Paul rebuked this behavior in 1 Corinthians chapter 11 verses 21 through 22: ". . .when you are eating, some of you go ahead with your own private suppers. As a result, one person remains hungry and another gets drunk. Don't you have homes to eat and drink in? Or do you despise the church of God by humiliating those who have nothing?" To modern day Christians, the description of hunger and intoxication in this passage sounds foreign in regards to the Lord's Supper, but the early church celebrated the Lord's Supper with large banquets. When the Lord's Supper was observed within the Corinthian's homes, the rich and privileged were permitted to eat first often leaving nothing for the poor. This self-centeredness was also seen by their failure to collect relief funds for the needy Christians in Jerusalem even though they had promised to do so. Paul had instructed them to take up this collection even before he wrote 1 Corinthians, but by the time he sent his second letter to them (2 Corinthians), they still had not completed it. Listen to Paul's exhortation to them regarding this matter: "Last year you were the first not only to give but also to have the desire to do so. Now finish the work, so that your eager willingness to do it may be matched by your completion of it" (2 Corinthians 8:10-11).

Jesus sought out those who were on the fringe of society; the marginal who are often dismissed as unimportant or not measuring up to the hierarchy's standards. He sought them out by going to where they were – he didn't always expect them to come to him. Jeffery Kingry appropriately questions, "That any Christian should consider others inferior and refuse social intercourse with them (a believer of a different ethnic group) is especially strange in view of the fact that Christ, despite his dignity and status, did not -- refuse to eat with even the lowliest of sinners (Mark. 2:16). If he was willing to eat with sinners like us, how could we imagine ourselves too good to eat with any man? (Parenthesis mine)."[12] To understand the outrage that Jesus' dining would have on the upper echelon of society one must understand what these outcasts represented. John Grassmick sheds some light on this passage. "Eating with Jesus were many tax collectors. . .and 'sinners,' a technical term for common people regarded by the Pharisees as untaught in the Law, who did not abide by rigid pharisaic standards. For Jesus and His disciples to share a meal (an expression of trust and fellowship) with them"[13] would be to offend the teachers of the Law (who were the Pharisees). Jesus had broken the oral tradition and became, what the Pharisees considered to be, ceremonially unclean, by eating with those who were on the outside of acceptable and dignified society.

Christ humbled himself so that he would draw people to himself. He "earned" the right (in the eyes of these sinners and tax collectors) because he met them where they were at and demonstrated his love to them. How then can we accept Christ's hospitality, yet refuse hospitality to another? We, too, need to go where others are and not expect them to come to us, for if they do not come, we have our excuse for not reaching out to those in need. It should not be missed that Jesus was not concerned with what his friends (his disciples) would think of his actions. Although the gospels say nothing about their reaction, it could be assumed that they were taken aback by his behavior. Jesus loved people so much that he was willing to jeopardize everything: his security, his stature, his reputation, his life. Jesus transcends ethnicity and cultures and economic status and educational experience and, yes, even religious backgrounds. He risked the stigma that was attached to someone who would associate with the fringe of society. Jesus died for the Islamic radical even as he did the American humanist. There is a lesson in this type of risk-taking. . ..to wander away from what is safe and comfortable and to build relationships with people who appear different from you and to love them – that's risky – but to do so is to win the bigger prize.

IMITATION IS THE SINCEREST FORM OF OBEDIENCE

The theme of the first thirteen verses of Romans chapter 15 is God's righteousness revealed in people's transformed lives by imitating Christ. "May the God who gives endurance and encouragement give you the same attitude of mind toward each other that Christ Jesus had, so that with one mind and one voice you may glorify the God and Father of our Lord Jesus Christ. Accept one another, then, just as Christ accepted you. . ." (vv. 5-7a). Why should we accept others? ". . .in order to bring praise to God (v 7b). The Christian must never forget the incredible fact that they were accepted by their Lord Jesus, and it was when believers were "powerless" (5:6, literally 'weak'), "ungodly" (5:6), "sinners" (5:8), and "enemies" (5:10) that he accepted them! Certainly Christians can receive others who differ from them in the color God chose for their skin!

In the second greatest book I've ever read, "The Moral Vision of the New Testament," Richard Hayes says this about imitating Christ: "As interpreted by Paul, the call to 'imitate Christ' means that the community is to forswear seeking its own self-defined freedom in order to render service to others, especially to the 'weak.' If it is necessary to give up what appear to be reasonable rights or privileges – for example, the freedom to eat certain foods – for the sake of others, then those who are in Christ should readily relinquish these rights, just as Christ surrendered his divine prerogatives and suffered death on the cross in order to save those who are weak and helpless under the power of sin."[14] The "weak" can also be seen as the powerless in our society; those who do not have a voice or the resources to change the circumstances in which they find themselves. Hayes goes on to point out that "Paul's call to imitate Christ is addressed to the community of faith, not just individuals."[15]

In the previous chapter I briefly mentioned Spiritual Civil Engineers, a term I use to describe believers who consciously build bridges in an attempt to unite people. Christians need to be in the business of building reconciliation bridges by actively seeking tactical opportunities which unite ethnic groups, not divide us. It is important to realize that in addition to skin color, it is also the chasm of economics which segregates us. The "have-nots" or "under-resourced" are often ignored by the "haves," and this is not just within our secular society; we see it within the local area church. Many affluent Christians are eager to hoard their wealth, building larger barns and storehouses to accumulate more and more possessions (Luke 12:13-21). I've heard them use the excuse that the Bible calls Christians to plan ahead so that they will not be a financial burden to others. The truth of that matter is that economic disparity is more complicated than that and the American structure of social and economic justice is insufferably inept. Those financially comfortable Christians who are consciously oblivious to the poor are those who have been deceived by their idol of mammon and as a result, secretly find their security in those treasures which will rot and deteriorate (Matthew 6:19). When the stock market crashes, which it will once again, these are the same people who are devastated and stressed over the loss of their precious god who promised financial security. The true God calls these people fools. The real scary thing is that many of these people don't even realize that they have replaced God with money and continue to go through the motions of being a Christian when, in the depths of their heart, they have little interest in pleasing Christ. The true evil of pride is that the more prideful you become, the less you realize it. It's a delusion that affects wealthy Christians as well as poor ones.

Jesus spoke often about the poor and exemplified a life where we are to love and care for the poor and those who find themselves on the fringe of society. "For I was hungry and you gave me something to eat, I was thirsty and you gave me something to drink, I was a stranger and you invited me in, I needed clothes and you clothed me, I was sick and you looked after me, I was in prison and you came to visit me. . . Truly I tell you, whatever you did for one of the least of these brothers and sisters of mine, you did for me" (Matthew 25:35, 36, 40b). It is no secret that much of the minority community is still suffering from limited opportunities, poor primary and secondary education, limited skill training and even, in some cases, appropriate Christian mentors. This has been brought on first by immoral laws and then by an oppressive and exclusive mindset by many of those whites who have traditionally held power.

In a recent interview with Rev. Craig Garriott (FCF), a multi-ethnic church located in the Pen Lucy community of Baltimore, he talked about the need to make sure the under-resourced people are being lifted-up and stated that the economic challenges still tend to be a greater hurdle for African Americans. By addressing people's material, physical, and financial needs first, we earn trust and respect, allowing us to attempt racial reconciliation within the church." Rev. Stan Long, co-pastor of FCF, added that "It is easier to reconcile the races than it is the economic barriers."[16] Until the inner city poor see how much we care, they will not care about how or why we are trying to integrate the church.

Henri Nouwen explains that our unconditional love for others is also how many lost people are drawn to Christianity. "Jesus' whole life was a witness to his Father's love, and Jesus calls his followers to carry on that witness in his Name. We, as followers of Jesus, are sent into this world to be visible signs of God's unconditional love. Thus, we are judged not first of all by what we say but by what we live. When people say of us, 'See how they love each other,' they catch a glimpse of the Kingdom of God that Jesus announced and are drawn to it as by a magnet." The apostle Paul echoed this sentiment, exhorting believers to "Share with the Lord's people who are in need. Practice hospitality" (Romans 12:13). Like the popular song the Jesus Freaks of the late 60s and 70s used to sing, "We Are One in the Spirit" (1966), where the emphasis on living a conspicuous Christian life was magnified in the line ". . .and they'll know we are Christians by our love."[17]

Christians are to mimic Christ. We are to copy, resemble, and take on the appearance of Christ in all that we do. The apostle Paul drives this point home in several of his letters to the various churches throughout his ministry. "Be *imitators* of God, therefore, as dearly loved children and live a life of love, just as Christ loved us and gave himself up for us as a fragrant offering and sacrifice to God" (Ephesians 5:1). Just as a child imitates his parents, so should a Christian imitate their Heavenly Father. "You became *imitators* of us and of the Lord; in spite of severe suffering, you welcomed the message with the joy given by the Holy Spirit. And so *you became a model* to all the believers in Macedonia and Achaia" (1

Thessalonians 1:6, emphasis mine). The Thessalonian Christians imitated the apostles who were imitating Christ, in spite of their trials and tribulations, as he restates in chapter 2.[18] " . . .and we also thank God continually because, when you received the word of God, which you heard from us, you accepted it not as the word of men, but as it actually is, the word of God, which is at work in you who believe. For you, brothers, became *imitators* of God's churches in Judea, which are in Christ Jesus. . ." (1 Thessalonians 2:14). From the world's eyes, if it walks like a duck, and quacks like a duck. . .well, you get the picture.

In the New Testament, servanthood and imitating Christ are often associated with suffering. If we place others before ourselves it will cost us something. It may cost us time, stature, and money, and in some cases, much more. There lies the reason why many fail to serve others obediently. If we are to serve our brothers and sisters of color, it will cost us something but, as we all know, anything that is of value is worth the investment. When it comes to suffering, Christ is our example. "To this you were called, because Christ suffered for you, leaving you an *example*, that you should follow in his steps" 1 Peter 2:21 (emphasis mine). The passage goes on to say that Christ did not retaliate when treated with contempt and hatred which led to his murder, all this just "so that we might die to sins and live for righteousness" (vv.24b). As we emulate Christ, we grow in our sanctification and we are able to forgive others just as God in Christ forgave us (Ephesians 4:32). Lack of ethnic reconciliation has a lot to do with history, which we'll look at in the next chapter. Painful memories make it difficult to forgive and even more difficult to associate with those who have hurt you, yet that is what we are called to do. When we step out in faith to trust God by our obedience, our reward both on earth and in heaven will be great!

FAITH = SUBMISSION + OBEDIENCE

The irony of Christ's commandment to love and serve others is that it *is* the remedy for a joyless Christian life. The reluctance of many who refuse to be obedient in serving is, in part, because they feel it will take the "fun" or "joy" out of life. To them it is a grudgingly difficult chore which sucks any enjoyment from their daily life, but this can't be farther from the truth. It is in serving others and obedience to Christ that true and complete joy and peace are found. There is also a failure to diagnose the sin of pride properly; not the "I am better than you," superiority form of pride, but the "woe is me," inferiority form of pride which is just as self-absorbed. In fact, for those suffering from non-biological/chemical depression, the cure is found in serving others. By taking the focus and energy off of ourselves and placing it on others we will be blessed and healed from our self-focused sorrow. I like how The Message translates Matthew 5:7. "You're blessed when you care. At the moment of being 'care-full,' you find yourselves cared for." Christians who lack the joy that God intended and wished for us to experience are the same Christians who fail to live out a life that seeks justice and one that is obsessed with generosity. They fail to see that if Christians do not care for the poor, no one else will. . .including our government. It is not someone else's problem; it is your problem and mine. We must stop hoarding our wealth and making bogus excuses for accumulating more "stuff" and give our money away until it hurts. This is the type of sacrificial love that puts others before ourselves. It is selflessness. It is Christlikeness.

In Paul's letter to the younger protégé, Timothy, he addresses the great responsibility wealthy Christians have to help their poor brothers and sisters. "Command those who are rich in this present world not to be arrogant nor to put their hope in wealth, which is so uncertain, but to put their hope in God, who richly provides us with everything for our enjoyment. Command them to do good, to be rich in good deeds, and to be generous and willing to share. In this way they will lay up treasure for themselves as a firm foundation for the coming age, so that they may take hold of the life that is truly life" (1 Timothy 6:17-19). This is a reflection of Christ's words that ". . . everyone who has been given much, much will be demanded; and from the one who has been entrusted with much, much more will be asked" (Luke 12:48). The affluent Western Christians, of whom there are many, are commanded to be incredibly generous with their wealth.

Many people have been inspired by the life testimony of Jim Elliot. Jim, a missionary to Ecuador, was killed by Waodani warriors along with his four companions. Jim understood well the need to "layup your treasures in heaven" (Matthew 6:19-21). His journal entry for October 28, 1949, expresses his belief that working for the kingdom of God was more important than his life. "He is no fool who gives what he cannot keep to gain what he cannot lose."[19]

There is an experience of close intimacy and holy love, which can only be experienced through obedience to God. Christ's teaching in John 14:23 reflects the expectation of obedience as an expression of our love for the Father and Son. "Jesus replied, "Anyone who loves me will obey my teaching. My Father will love them, and we will come to them and make our home with them." To love Jesus is to obey Jesus. G.L. Borchert states that John is not making a legalistic plea for keeping the Mosaic Law, but "rather adopting a profound sense of obedient servanthood modeled on the servant pattern of the Son with the Father (John 5:19). Loving Jesus is therefore a commitment to the 'way' of Jesus."[20] Spence adds his beautiful prospective on this passage.

". . .instead of saying, 'I will love him, and manifest myself,' he added, **We will come**– the Father and I – to him, and take up our abode, make for ourselves a resting **Place in his dwelling**. . . the analogous and wonderful parallel in Rev. 3:20 ('Here I am! I stand at the door and knock. If anyone hears my voice and opens the door, I will come in and eat with him, and he with me.') There is a clear utterance of Divine self-consciousness. It is worthy of note that such an expression as this sounds a profounder depth of that consciousness than any phrase. . .already delivered. Apart from the stupendous corroborative facts elsewhere on record, this seems, to mere human experience, either awfully true or infinitely blasphemous. *The Father and I* will come together in the power of the Spirit, and *we* will dwell within the loving and obedient soul. This phrase suggests the mystical union of the Divine Personality with that of those who have entered into spiritual relation with Christ through love and obedience."[21] (Parenthesis mine).

The last words Jesus spoke on this earth to his disciples were a reminder for them to teach the world to obey everything Jesus had commanded them to do (Matt. 28:19 -20; Acts 1:8). Certainly some doubted (at first) as to the authenticity of Jesus' appearance. "They worshiped Him, but some doubted" (v. 17). It wasn't the Resurrection they doubted, it was whether this was truly Jesus, however the "Great Commission" was received and extended through the simple equation of faith = submission *and* obedience. Unless *they* obeyed Christ, they could never expect others to obey Him. It was a prerequisite for the official commissioning. "Therefore go and make disciples of all nations, baptizing them in the name of the Father and of the Son and of the Holy Spirit, and teaching them to *obey everything I have commanded you.* And surely I am with you always, to the very end of the age" (v. 19, emphasis mine). Jesus' commissioning of his disciples had an all-encompassing spectrum that included all peoples throughout the world. In Acts 1:8 he tells them, "But you will receive power when the Holy Spirit comes on you; and you will be my witnesses in Jerusalem, and in all Judea and Samaria, and to the ends of the earth." Stan Long (FCF) comments on the way many churches today interpret that command. Long says "Most churches think of their 'Jerusalem' and the rest of the world, but not their 'Samaria' and 'Judea' right next door." We send missionaries halfway across the globe to build relationships with these "foreign" people while neglecting those a few towns over who also need reconciling relationships with God.

Sometimes I try to think how Jesus would act and react to life in twenty-first century America. Without a doubt, his heart would be broken. The nation which began on the premise of "one nation under God" has become many nations without God. The United States is now the largest exporter of pornography in the world, has murdered over 54,559,615 innocent babies since abortion became legalized in 1973,[22] and has been an ever-increasing immoral society since we decided to kick God out of our schools in 1962. This great nation which sent more missionaries to the farthest corners of the globe than anyone else is now the recipient of scores of missionaries from third-world countries. The United States of America pledges that "all men are created equal," and certainly we have made great strides in the public arena to embrace that ideal, yet the church remains segregated (actually even more segregated) than it was at the end of the Civil War in 1865. I wonder what type of church Jesus would go to if he was in America today. Would he find a church/synagogue where only Messianic Jews[23] gathered? Would he associate only with people who were of the same ethnicity as him? I doubt it. Jesus fought bigotry as some of his greatest battles were with the religious leaders of that society who practiced a religious elitism. He would most certainly want to worship his Father with those who are representative of the kingdom; people from all ethnic backgrounds, from all heritages, from the four corners of the earth; the same type of people he came to earth to die for.

NOTES:

CHAPTER 4: CHRIST-LIKE MEANS "LIKE" CHRIST

---

[1]   For Jesus to touch a leper would be to risk ritual defilement due to rabbinic regulations.

[2]   Howard Thurman, *Jesus and the Disinherited* (Boston: Beacon Press, 1976), 7.

[3]   Ibid., 8.

[4]   D.L. Akin, "1, 2, 3 John," in *The New American Commentary* Vol. 38: 96. (Nashville: Broadman & Holman Publishers, 2001).

[5]   Zane C. Hodges, "1 John," *The Bible Knowledge Commentary*, eds., John F. Walvoord & Roy B. Zuck (Wheaton, Il.: Victor Books, 1985), 891-892.

[6]   See also the Apostle Paul's analogy of grafting in Romans 11: 17-24.

[7]   G. L. Borchert, "John 12–21," *The New American Commentary* Vol. 25B. (Nashville: Broadman & Holman Publishers, 2002).

[8]   C. Blomberg, "Matthew," The *New American Commentary* Vol. 22. (Nashville: Broadman & Holman Publishers, 1992).

[9]   Ibid.

[10]   Henri Nouwen, *Bread for the Journey* (New York: HarperOne, 1997), December 26.

[11]   H.H. Hobbs, *My favorite illustrations* (Nashville, TN: Broadman Press, 1990), 25.

[12]   Jeffery Kingry, "The Christian and Race Relations," *Truth Magazine* XXI: 34, (September 1, 1977): 536-539; available from http://www.truthmagazine.com/archives/volume21/TM021253.html; accessed 17 Aug 2012.

[13]   John D. Grassmick, "Mark," *The Bible Knowledge Commentary*, eds., John F. Walvoord & Roy B. Zuck (Wheaton, Il.: Victor Books, 1985), 113.

[14]   Hays, *Moral Vision of the New Testament*, 452.

[15]   Ibid.

[16]   Rev. Craig Garriott & Rev. Stan Long , interview by author, 23 June 2012, recording held by author.

[17]   Peter Scholtes, "They'll Know We Are Christians By Our Love" [doc. on-line]; available from http://www.invubu.com/quotes/songs/show/Peter_Scholtes/They'll_Know_We_Are_Christians_By_Our_Love.html; accessed from 19 Nov 2012.

[18]   We see Paul exhorting his readers to imitate himself as he imitates Christ (1 Corinthians 4:16 and 11:1), perhaps because these young Christians did not have

the benefit of the New Testament Scriptures which provide the Spirit's teaching ministry of Christ.

[19]   Wikipedia states that "This is the quote that is most often attributed to Elliot, but apparently it is very close to the English nonconformist preacher Philip Henry (1631–1696) who said 'He is no fool who parts with that which he cannot keep, when he is sure to be recompensed with that which he cannot lose'" available from http://en.wikipedia.org/wiki/Jim_Elliot.

[20]   G.L. Borchert, "John 12–21," The New American Commentary Vol. 25B. (Nashville: Broadman & Holman Publishers, 2002).

[21]   H. D. M. Spence-Jones, ed., *St. John*, The Pulpit Commentary Vol. II. (New York: Funk & Wagnalls Company, 1909).

[22]   Christian Life Resources, "U.S. Abortion Statistics By Year (1973-Current)" [doc. on-line]; available from http://www.christianliferesources.com/article/u-s-abortion-statistics-by-year-1973-current-1042; ; accessed from 11 Oct 2012.

[23]   A Messianic Jew is a Jew who believes in the "messiahship" and divinity of Jesus.

5

A PERSPECTIVE IN
BLACK AND WHITE

*Though I am free and belong to no one, I have made myself a
slave to everyone, to win as many as possible. . . I have become all
things to all people so that by all possible means
I might save some.*
1 Corinthians 9: 19, 22b

*You, then, why do you judge your brother or sister? Or why do you
treat them with contempt? For we will all stand before
God's judgment seat.*
Romans 14:10

*Do not deceive yourselves. If any of you think you are wise by the
standards of this age, you should become "fools" so that you may
become wise. For the wisdom of this world is
foolishness in God's sight.*
1 Corinthians 3: 18-19a

*O*ne's perspective is always painted by the brush of life experience, environment, and immediate needs. Our view on politics, relationships, and even religion, is filtered by the "me" lens which can be inherently dangerous and misguided, giving us a warped view of reality and deceiving us from obtaining a Christ-like perspective. It is more than difficult for me, a white, middle-aged male, to have an accurate perspective of the black experience in the United States, regardless of how open-minded and willing I am. I can, however, learn to understand the African American perspective better through interaction with them and developing *meaningful* (not superficial) crosscultural relationships. As these friendships grow, I earn respect and the right to ask hard questions and to have tough questions asked of me, but this takes an investment of time and a willingness to be vulnerable. If one lives in a geographic area that is culturally and ethnically diverse, then as a disciple of Christ, one should seek out a church which is representative of that community. If there isn't one, we need to help change the church to make it one that is! We need to have a more spatial perspective, a perspective which is expansive, not inwardly focused; one that incorporates the geographic and social factors around that area to bring proper reconciliation to the people of that region. If we refuse to help create a church which is ethnically representative of its community, we fail at building a healthy church body and instead have one which is flawed internally, attacked by racial pathogens. As Rev. Craig Garriott (FCF) so aptly puts it, "I need this for my own sanctification – for my own maturity! I need this because this is the center of the gospel – where God is moving. You have to feel a gospel imperative. Until those lights come on, the serious work of racial reconciliation isn't going to be there." Garriott's co-pastor Rev. Stan Long adds, "People are grounding that into the simplicity of the cross, not by sociological compulsion. . .in other words, the cross demands it!" We can attempt racial reconciliation through studying the interpretive macro-level understanding of social action by focusing on those social structures which shape our society, but our motivation will always be lacking. If not for the cross, then why?

If I continue to try to understand African Americans and other ethnic groups by attempting to have empathy for their unique challenges from solely my own sterile perspective, I am then committed to failure. My perspective has no possibility of being untainted. If the truth be known, all human beings have some degree of prejudice within themselves. This should come as no surprise to any of us. We are all infected children of Adam and Eve and, unfortunately, carry with us some of the characteristics of our earthly father thanks to our imputed sin, that sin which we inherited from our "father," Adam. There is an innate (sinful) element within us all that warns us whenever we meet someone who appears different than us, whether that difference be skin color, dialect, educational background, or even age. We pre-judge people simply because of appearance. It can be gray hair and wrinkles, tattoos, piercings, dress (low-cut blouses, low-riding pants that expose underwear or even outdated clothing).

WHAT, ME, PREJUDICED?

Failure to recognize our sinful inclination to judge others based on our definition of culture, developed solely through personal life experience (which may be incredibly limited), is to assure that bias and prejudice will be well fostered in our lives. Pre-judging through assumptions is incredibly dangerous and we should be protected against our tendency to do so. Case in point, if you happen to live in an all-white neighborhood and you were to see a young African American man walking down your street, what would be the first thought in your mind? We must evaluate our hearts with the supernatural help of the Holy Spirit in order to bring clarity to that which promotes hatred and suppresses love for others.

It wasn't until I began to grow in my faith and knowledge of Jesus Christ and surrender to His will that God could begin the metamorphosis I so desperately needed in my life. It wasn't until Christ dethroned *me* that I could even begin to see people as He does (yet it continues to be a lifelong process), but this is not a one-and-done event. Sanctification is a lifelong process which requires a daily surrender and commitment to Christ. The Holy Spirit can/will only begin to change us when we humbly yield to his direction and stop trying to thwart his work.

My story is one that morphed into bigotry at an early age and, through the supernatural work of Christ in my life, brought me to a place where I have had success in loving others, regardless of their physical appearance. But before I go on to tell that story; I believe it is crucial to acknowledge that although I have become more culturally sensitive, I still possess elements of prejudice. That is a painful admission for me simply because, like all of Adam's children, I struggle with the fact that I am not quite as "good" as I want to believe I am. The killing of SELF is a daily chore and only possible when we allow the Holy Spirit to have his way with us. Otherwise we allow pride to go unchecked in our lives.

In their chapter on "Our Multicultural Challenge," the Breckenridges brusquely state that "True ministry within a multicultural context must begin with the admission that each of us is prejudiced."[1] This is not to say it is always a deliberate, conscious, obvious action towards a culture different than our own, rather it is the expression of a life lived from a mono-cultural perspective, polluted by sin. It is acting in a manner which is insensitive and oblivious to how other cultures may receive what I am saying or doing. For example, if I am responsible for the children's Sunday education (Sunday school) at my church and I choose a curriculum that was written exclusively for white audiences, ignoring the cultural differences of the black or Hispanic, or Asian, or Middle Eastern experience, I exercise a prejudice whether intentional or not. If the Breckenridges are correct in their assessment, then Christians need to pay particular attention to these sinful tendencies.

Welcoming anyone who is new to our gatherings is something that many churches are becoming better at doing. Most churches have assigned "greeters" who welcome visitors to their worship service, but there is still enough of an exclusion mentality in churches that sends a message that "you are not one of us." Over the years I've visited a fair amount of stereotypical suburban churches where my wife and I have *not* felt very welcomed and, as a result, felt a little out-of-place, though we were among fellow believers. . .. . .and this was when everyone looked pretty much like us! Just imagine how we would have felt if our skin was a different color than the rest of the congregation!

POWER

As stated in an earlier chapter, Christians need to take conscious and deliberate steps to integrate those evangelical churches that exist in an ethnically diverse community so that ethnic reconciliation might become a possibility. The awareness needed then, is one of inclusivity, not exclusivity. The local church must be an authentic representation of its surrounding community. In some cases, being mono-cultural is a realistic representation of its community. There are areas in our country where the culture *is* but one ethnicity and for those churches; an awareness of diverse cultures and ethnic groups may only come through short-term missions, perhaps to urban areas which traditionally are a melting pot of diversity.

If the American evangelical church does not reconcile with their brothers and sisters of varying skin color they will have failed at one of the great opportunities God has given the American church. The "browning of America" is an uncomplicated fact. African American, Hispanic and Asian populations "continue to outpace Anglo population's much slower growth."[2] In an interview in Christianity Today, D. Michael Lindsay, President of Gordon College, states, "The browning of America is going to be significantly felt in American evangelicalism because both of these populations (Hispanic and Asian) are more religiously committed than their white counterparts" (parenthesis mine).[3] In the same article, Phillip Ryken, president of Wheaton College, adds, "We want to have relationships that live out what it means to work, play, worship, and study together with a full expression of what it means to belong to the kingdom of God."[4]

It is understandable that many older people of varying ethnicities have a strong desire to preserve their cultural identity so that the younger generation doesn't lose that distinctiveness. That challenge is huge, especially in first generation Americans. Any serious discussion regarding ethnic reconciliation must include some careful anthropological, cross-cultural analysis. The popular author and speaker Tony Campolo shares that "Being black, white, Asian, Hispanic proves to be more than just a difference in skin color. There are cultural traditions, language forms, value systems that are very distinct within each of these groups."[5] Rev. Stan Long (FCF) states that when it comes to ethnic integration within the church there is still more resistance from the African American community than the white community. "The African American church has historically been where we (African Americans) have had power and decision-making – where we have done things, not only scripturally, but culturally."[6] Rev. Long's white co-pastor, Craig Garriott echoes this perspective. "Historically, because of institutional racism, African Americans have had to accommodate, all week long, to a foreign power system. Church has become a safe place of cultural affirmation and for those African Americans to then give that up, to subject themselves to white ignorance, their heritage, and their culture, that takes a huge maturity. . ."[7]

My friend, Rev. Tyrone Perkins, pastor of Trenton, New Jersey's Westside Bible Baptist suggests that there may be a shift in generational perspectives toward assimilating into a church dominated by an ethnic group unlike oneself. "While this may be true of older African American Christians, I don't think it is generally true of the younger generation who have much more experience existing in a diverse environment. My sense is that it is easier for an African American to attend a predominantly white church than for a white Christian to attend a predominantly African American church."[8]

The realization of power within the church is nothing to be overlooked. It is absurd to assume that African Americans will feel welcome in white assemblies as brethren in Christ, without churches relinquishing positions of power, which include deacons, elders, and pastors. Here is where a genuine effort to understand another's perspective will prevent a "trial and error" approach which significantly extends the learning curve. I have no doubt that whites would feel the same way if they were integrating into a predominately black congregation.

Certainly, there has been movement towards conciliatory relations between ethnic groups since World War II, as the ice-hard glacier of privilege and power in the old Protestant establishment had begun to be chiseled and melted away bringing with it an embracing of the nation's growing diversity. But why are we not experiencing this diversity within unity in our churches across the nation? Our churches will remain segregated until we welcome black men and women into white assemblies *and* offer them positions of leadership, power and responsibility at all levels. This is one reason why Faith Christian Fellowship has experienced some success in their efforts in becoming a diverse congregation. Rev. Garriott adds, "Historically, African Americans have been suspect that whites would not sit under the leadership of an African American, but that is changing."

ECONOMICS

The economic challenges still tend to be a greater hurdle for African Americans and, very possibly, the greatest obstacle standing in the way of true reconciliation and unity of the ethnic groups within the American Evangelical Christian church. Community development is the key in creating a welcoming church environment for non-whites and it is crucial that the under-resourced people are being dignified and built-up. In fact, the economic chasm between the wealthy and the poor separates people of like skin color. Tony Campolo recently told me "When you stop to consider that, you recognize that even white people have difficulty worshiping together when differences in economic status are given consideration."

In the 1979 U.S. Catholic Bishops Pastoral Letter on Racism, the Catholic Church shed some light on the significant (and growing) impact that financial inequality places on what seems to be the irreconcilable differences between the ethnic groups.

"Racism and economic oppression are distinct but inter-related forces which dehumanize our society. Movement toward authentic justice demands a simultaneous attack on both evils. Our economic structures are undergoing fundamental changes which threaten to intensify social inequalities in our nation. We are entering an era characterized by limited resources, restricted job markets and dwindling revenues. In this atmosphere, the poor and racial minorities are being asked to bear the heaviest burden of the new economic pressures. This new economic crisis reveals an unresolved racism that permeates our society's structures and resides in the hearts of many among the majority. Because it is less blatant, this subtle form of racism is in some respects even more dangerous — harder to combat and easier to ignore."[9]

This is not to say that poverty is foreign to crossing ethnic lines, for poverty has always refrained from discriminating. We are only saying that the economic chasm may actually be greater than the ethnic chasm. There must be a sense of ownership when empowering someone to break the chains of poverty. Jesus told a parable about servants who are awaiting their master's return. Although there are several lessons which can be drawn from this parable, there is a basic premise of godly stewardship for the faithful Christian - not only monetarily, but of all gifts and talents God has given us. Jesus ends the story my stating that ". . .everyone who has been given much, much will be demanded; and from the one who has been entrusted with much, much more will be asked" (Luke 12:36-48). This statement is a bit more complicated than just writing a check, appeasing one's conscience by thinking you have done a noble thing and then forgetting about the disenfranchised. Those who have much must provide the resources, but a hand-out without allowing the individual to participate in the solution is nothing more than a band-aid on a life-threatening wound. You are barely treating the symptoms, not the cause. The government continues to throw more and more money at the problem of poverty without finding practical ways to help the disenfranchised break the chain of dependence through education and job training *and access.* Throwing money at the problem of poverty does a fine job of appeasing our conscience, but does nothing to rectify the problem. It provides administrative jobs to people who often have a negative attitude toward the disenfranchised.

There's an old proverb you've probably heard before, "Give a man a fish and you feed him for a day. Teach a man to fish and you feed him for a lifetime."[10] Human nature has a tendency not to take care of anything which is given without personal cost to us. It's true with others and it is true with you and me. I did not grow up in a wealthy family. We always had what we needed, but seldom received the extra "things" children always want. However, one of the greatest Davis traditions was that when each child reached their 9th birthday we would receive a new bicycle. Being the youngest of four and having grown accustomed to hand-me-downs, this tradition was particularly special to me. But soon I grew apathetic towards a possession that cost me nothing. As much as I loved that cherry-red Huffy, I soon stopped using its kickstand and made a habit of jumping off the moving bike when I arrived at my destination, allowing it to crash head-on into bushes, a fence, or worse!

A few years later, 10 speed bicycles became all the rage, so I rode my 3 speed Huffy over to the Keswick Bicycle shop in Glenside, the next town over, and inspected the wide variety of 10 speeds they had on display. . ..and there it was, the most beautiful thing I had ever seen. . .a 10 speed Schwinn Super Sport in sunset orange. I drooled! I went home to share the wonderful news of my discovery with my parents only to have the air taken out of my balloon. They had a family "policy" and they were going to stick by it. One new bicycle per lifetime! It wouldn't be fair to my siblings if I received two bicycles when they were only given one (not to mention the expense). There was no such thing as an allowance in the Davis household. The theory was that we children were part of a family unit which was greater than any one person. Contributing to the welfare of the group was expected, without compensation, and this would instill a healthy work ethic in us children. It was clear that if I was going to obtain this prize bicycle, I was going to have to save my money and buy it myself. The cost, $100! I would have to work for it, and work I did! I cut lawns, raked leaves, chopped wood and shoveled snow. I saved. I did without the summer indulgence of a Jack Frost ice cream cone. I was dedicated. And finally, one day, I had the funds to secure that Schwinn Super Sport, and do you know what? I babied that bike. I polished the chrome. I washed and waxed it. I even used the kickstand. I took great care of it because it was my pride and joy *because it cost me something!* We are all that way. We take better care of things that cost us something. Perhaps that is the reason why so many Christians take the price that was paid for our salvation for granted. Yes, it cost us nothing, but it cost God's Son a great deal!

We've all seen the condition that much of the public housing is in. I can remember driving past some of these high rises in Philadelphia where windows would be boarded up from being broken and vandalized. That scene is in contrast with what is happening at Habitat for Humanity. Habitat defines itself as "a nonprofit, ecumenical Christian housing ministry that has helped to build over 500,000 decent, affordable houses and served 2.5 million people worldwide. In addition to a down payment and monthly mortgage payments, homeowners invest hundreds of hours of their own labor into building their Habitat house and the houses of others. Habitat houses are sold to partner families at no profit and financed with affordable loans."[11]

Caleb Rosado's article on understanding prejudice and racism through economics offers a prophetic quote made at the beginning of the twentieth century and remains true today:

"In 1903 W. B. E. Dubois, the great African American writer and sociologist, declared in his book, The Souls of Black Folk, that 'the problem of the twentieth century is the problem of the color-line, the relation of the darker to the lighter races of men in Asia and Africa, in America and the islands of the sea.' Fifty years later, however, he altered his views with the realization that the real problems were economic. "Today I see more clearly than yesterday that back of the problem of race and color, lies a greater problem which both obscures and implements it: and that is the fact that so many civilized persons are willing to live in comfort even if the price of this is poverty, ignorance and disease of the majority of their fellowmen."[12]

As Christians we are called to a life of inequality, in that all others should be viewed as *more important* than ourselves. Indifference towards those who are economically oppressed is a sinful approach to a large group of people about whom Jesus cared deeply. It is simply too easy to become oblivious to the issues that concern and affect the inner city. We are called to a life of sacrificial giving and love which is demonstrated, at the very least, toward the poor and disenfranchised. A helping hand is not that if it is done to appease one's conscience or under structural pressure. In America we have somehow adopted the mentality that it is the government's responsibility to care for the poor. Nothing could be farther from a biblical view, for the Bible consistently teaches that believers have a moral obligation to care for the poor. Deuteronomy 14:28 - 15:11 speaks specifically about lending without interest and even forgiveness of debt should the debtor default on the loan. Verse 4 goes as far to state". . .there should be no poor among you, for in the land the Lord your God is giving you to possess as your inheritance, he will richly bless you." Could any American question how prodigiously God has blessed us?

I disagree with Mark Galli, *Christianity Today's* senior managing editor, when he says "the church cannot defeat poverty. . . Doing our little part makes very little difference when it comes to large-scale poverty."[13] If the 200 million American Christians would combine their efforts I have little doubt that the church's "return on investment" would dwarf the government's wasteful attempts. It is the church, not government, which should provide for the needs of the poor. Due to their divine motivation, ideally they are better suited to supply for both the physical and the spiritual needs of the poor and disenfranchised. The government has done an abysmal job in attempting to relieve the symptoms and the causes of poverty in our country. The continuing mentality in Washington to throw more and more money towards the problem is not working. It never has and it never will!

We cannot turn away from the fact that welfare is more alleviative than curative. Whether deliberate or not, it creates generations of dependent poor, ensuring that the vicious cycle continues and their victims remain poor. It is more than possible that some politicians do not want these people to be freed from the bondage of welfare because the dependence upon these government social programs assures votes for re-election (and keeps many government workers employed). It's no secret that the vast numbers of those living under the poverty level are one- parent households. Simply put, keep the family together and you will reduce poverty significantly – to a level never before seen in our country! Our society has mocked the biblical description of the "traditional" family, even to the degree of creating numerous (popular) television shows that embrace and even support a picture of the "new normal" for American families. What once was the traditional two-parent family is now "abnormal."

The government simply has no incentive or intention to keep families intact, in fact, their policies actually penalize those financially challenged couples. It becomes pretty clear where the church needs to spend its time and energy. In an article on "Single-parent Families in Poverty," Ohio State University's Jacqueline Kirby writes:

"One of the most striking changes in family structure over the last twenty years has been the increase in single-parent families. In 1970, the number of single-parent families with children under the age of 18 was 3.8 million. By 1990, the number had more than doubled to 9.7 million. For the first time in history, children are more likely to reside in a single-parent family for reasons other than the death of a parent. One in four children is born to an unmarried mother, many of whom are teenagers. Another 40 percent of children under 18 will experience parental breakup.

Ninety percent of single-parent families are headed by females. Not surprisingly, single mothers with dependent children have the highest rate of poverty across all demographic groups (Olson & Banyard, 1993). Approximately 60 percent of U.S. children living in mother-only families are impoverished, compared with only 11 percent of two-parent families. The rate of poverty is even higher in African-American single-parent families, in which two out of every three children are poor."[14]

It's no surprise that the Democrats control the inner city politics, for they are the party that promotes government social programs. Of the 10 poorest cities in the United States, all have a Democrat mayor, yet the plight of the poor has not only failed to experience the slightest improvement, the chasm between poor and rich is widening. The government will tell you that the challenge in solving the poverty problem is one of finances. They simply do not have the monetary resources. That is a blatant lie. Throwing more and more money at the problem hasn't alleviated poverty one iota, as evident by how quickly the problem is growing. In his book on *How the Early Church practiced Charity*, Walter Brueggemann states "Upon receiving the Nobel Peace Prize, former president Jimmy Carter remarked that the 'growing gap between the rich and poor' is the most elemental problem facing the world economy."[15]

Republicans must accept some of the blame here as well. Just as the Democrats believe that creating more social programs and throwing more money at the poor will solve the problem, Republicans would prefer to ignore the plight of the poor, and although it is understandable that they would like to eliminate social programs which have been a dismal failure, Republicans offer no solution to helping the poor and disenfranchised and, in fact, many of their programs favor the rich at the expense of the poor.

The Federal government is an enabler of welfare-dependent people, many who have lost the desire or vision to seek employment. Why should they? Minimum wage provides less income than what the Department of Public Welfare offers. The government has developed a sub-society with an entitlement mentality. The truth is that the government is ill-equipped to help these people despite having vast resources. Instead of empowering the poor with skill sets and education, and access to jobs in order to succeed, they construct a nearly impermeable lid upon the federal cesspool of poverty which creates an apathetic group who have bought into an entitlement mentality. The cost of secondary education is immoral. In a country as rich with resources as the United States, an increasing number of bright young people having great potential either cannot find the resources to go to college or they fall into substantial debt in order to obtain their degree.

The church is best equipped to serve the poor, if for no other reason, because they are motivated by love for their Lord and Savior whom they choose to serve. But, as with any sensible solution, there are great challenges that hamper action and progress. We (America) would rather have a lottery or pass out welfare checks than to roll-up our sleeves and lend a real helping hand to the poor. Perhaps we need to do some soul-searching to expose the idols we hold close to our chests. For some of us, time and comfort are much more valuable to us than money. Getting actively involved with the plight of the poor would require vulnerability, eye contact and would eliminate our anonymity. A check is impersonal. Personal involvement is, well, personal. One of the problems with empowering the church to address and alleviate the growing problem of poverty is that the Christian faith is severely splintered into dozens of various sects. Instead of coordinating efforts between Catholics, Presbyterians, Methodists, Baptists, Lutherans, etc., each sect works independently, often duplicating their efforts and, because of limited resources, has a minimal impact. Galli correctly states that "What separates Christian Democrats and Christian Republicans is not their concern for the poor but rather their strategies for helping the poor."[16]

While Mark Galli and I can disagree on who best can address the plight of the poor, we can agree on the church's need to do more. Galli adds, "Ah, but people – those precious individuals embedded in a unique family and community – they are right in the church's sweet spot. No government can touch what the church can do here.

So while the government makes needed sweeping changes, the church is there to pick up the inevitable pieces of people trampled by government regulations, of people who get left behind, of people whom the government treats as mindless sheep, but whom the church knows have a Shepherd."[17]

Church tithing has become an increasingly difficult thing for Western Christians to practice as evident of the diminishing finances most churches face.[18] Even in the most affluent churches where cash flow is not an issue, you will find that the majority of congregants are giving less than 10% of their income. If you'd like to prove this to yourself, a simple algebraic exercise will reveal to you the pathetic lack of generosity within the church. Most churches publish what last week's giving was. Take the number of giving units[19] in your church and divide the monthly receivables into that number. For example, if a church has monthly receivables from the offering totaling $10,000 and they have 50 giving units, the monthly average giving margin per unit would be $200. Multiply that $200 by 12 months and you come up with $2400. If we take the tithe to represent 10% of one's gross income, we can deduce that the average yearly income of each giving unit is $24,000/year. I promise you will be amazed at how low an average income results from your calculations.

Years ago I was a member of a pretty affluent church with a large congregation where attenders lived in a very comfortable suburban environment. The giving, however, was not even close to being representative of the average lifestyle, but since it had such a large congregation, their revenue was substantial enough to provide a significant variety of ministries and "creature comforts." When you start doing the math you quickly realize how little most people are giving for the Lord's work. No wonder it is easier for a camel to go through the eye of a needle than for a rich man to enter heaven!

It is a remarkable thing to witness the re-assimilation to American culture that Christians experience when returning from short-term mission trips. The expenditure by Americans on frivolous things like pet costumes, crafts, toys, and non-essential clothing, when vast numbers of fellow third world Christians have no idea where their next meal will come from, brings clarity to how frivolous we each are. Sacrificial giving is most often seen in these poor people who are so quick to give the little they have to someone else. In the Gospel of Mark, Jesus sat and watched as people put their money into the temple treasury. The rich threw in large amounts of money *from their surplus* while a poor widow put in a few copper coins amounting to her life savings (12: 41-44). As disciples of Jesus we are not called to give a tithe, a 10% *token* from our bounty in order to appease our consciences. We are to give willingly, cheerfully, and without reservation (2 Corinthians 9:7). We are called to give sacrificially. To give out of our surplus costs us nothing. An offering is something offered as a sacrifice to God. It has to cost us something. Our expression of love towards our brothers and sisters must be a love of action which, when seeing a need, instinctively reacts generously as instigated by our new nature. This generosity should be natural and the need obvious to anyone who calls themselves a disciple of Jesus Christ. John reminds us, "This is how we know what love is: Jesus Christ laid down his life for us. And we ought to lay down our lives for our brothers and sisters. If anyone has material possessions and sees a brother or sister in need but has no pity on them, how can the love of God be in that person? Dear children, let us not love with words or speech but with actions and in truth" (1 John 3:16-18).

PERSPECTIVE EXPOSED IN OUR MOTIVES

The problem with poverty in America is, to a large degree, a spiritual problem, not a materialistic or political problem. Mother Theresa astutely observed that "When a poor person dies of hunger, it has not happened because God did not take care of him or her. It has happened because neither you nor I wanted to give that person what he or she needed. . ..You and I, we are the Church, no? We have to share with our people. Suffering today is because people are hoarding, not giving, not sharing. Jesus made it clear, "Whatever you do to the least of my brethren, you do it to me. Give a glass of water, you give it to me. Receive a little child, you receive me" (Matt. 25:45)."[20]

We must be careful with what truly motivates our actions. We must ask ourselves difficult questions and answer with truthfulness in order to expose why we are doing what we are doing and for whom we are doing it. Exposing our motives is often a painful exorcism of self-glorifying sin which is carefully crafted to appear as something holy, righteous, and sacrificial. Many of us deceive ourselves into thinking that we are serving others when, in reality, we are serving ourselves (and our needs) by "helping" others.

The Book of James takes a deliberate look at the Christian's motives toward a variety of actions, including poverty and wealth (1: 9-11). James tells us that poverty can be a means by which we grow spiritually and develop our Christian character. "Believers in humble circumstances ought to take pride in their high position. But the rich should take pride in their humiliation—since they will pass away like a wild flower" (1:9-10). The wealthy must remember that money and social prominence will wither away and their true wealth is only in their eternal inheritance through Jesus Christ. James began his book by telling his readers to "consider it pure joy. . .whenever you face trials. . . . .because (it) develops perseverance" and it is through this perseverance that we become "mature and complete, not lacking anything" (1: 2, 3b, 4b). So in light of these truths, who is in better spiritual condition, the poor or the rich? Jesus said "Again I tell you, it is easier for a camel to go through the eye of a needle than for a rich man to enter the kingdom of God" (Matthew 19:24). It is not money which defiles a man, it is the *love* of money (1 Timothy 6:10). Shame on the rich man who has the resources to relieve some of the poor man's suffering but instead sits in his castle counting his money. In his no nonsense and deliberate way of calling it as he sees it, James warns the rich oppressor. "Now listen, you rich people, weep and wail because of the misery that is coming on you. Your wealth has rotted, and moths have eaten your clothes. Your gold and silver are corroded. Their corrosion will testify against you and eat your flesh like fire. You have hoarded wealth in the last days. Look! The wages you failed to pay the workers who mowed your fields are crying out against you. The cries of the harvesters have reached the ears of the Lord Almighty. You have lived on earth in luxury and self-indulgence. You have fattened yourselves in the day of slaughter" (5: 1-5).

BEING A PATRIOT

Americans tend to be loyal and dedicated to their great country and most of them realize that they live in the greatest country this world has ever seen. They wear the label of being a patriot as a badge of honor. A patriot is someone who feels a strong support for his or her country and when Americans look at the great and generous things the United States has done throughout the world, we feel a sense of pride. But it should be noted that as Christians, our citizenship is not of this world. The apostle Paul reminds us that our citizenship is in heaven (Philippians 3:20) and Peter agrees.

"Dear friends, I urge you, as *aliens and strangers in the world*, to abstain from sinful desires, which war against your soul" (1 Peter 2:11, emphasis mine). Please do not misunderstand what I'm saying here. I previously shared that I served proudly in the United States military and I'm deeply grateful to live in this country that I love. There's no place on earth where I'd rather live, but my first allegiance is not to any country, earthly king (or president), or political philosophy, it is to my Creator and his Son, my Savior, who have prepared a kingdom for me and have offered me an incredible inheritance. It is not Jesus' ethnicity, cultural distinctiveness, nor his national identity which saves the lost individual, but his *divine nationality*, from above this world, which sanctions his title as Son of God. He *who died for all* gives life graciously to those who come to the cross and deny themselves. "Therefore I want you to know that God's salvation has been sent to the Gentiles, and they will listen!" (Acts 28:28). Our indigenous perspective must include the understanding that as God's pilgrim people he will accomplish a second exodus in bringing us home to him.

In his book, *"Has Christianity Failed You?"* Ravi Zacharias states, "The vision of God for humanity is that we might see his claim on us as an invitation to live and love, transcending all ethnic and cultural boundaries, not because Jesus is David's son, but because he is the instrument of power over all over power, of essential worth over political ideology, of human need over ethnic arrogance. He has eradicated every barrier of race and culture and position in life."[21] Allegiance to anything we make more important than Christ is not only a barrier, it is an idol. It is our reconciled relationship with Christ, and the power we have received through the Spirit, which allows us to reach across all manmade boundaries confidently to reconcile ourselves with others without surrendering our ethnic or cultural identity.

SOCIAL JUSTICE

The term "social justice" should be synonymous with the word "Christians." Concern which manifests itself in germane action for victims of economic, political, and social inequality should be a passion for all Christians. One of the ways the apostle Paul wanted believers to pursue righteousness, even to those outside the faith, was through family care. "Anyone who does not provide for their relatives, and especially for their own household, has denied the faith and is worse than an unbeliever" (1 Timothy 5:8). One's own "household" can easily be extended to include those within the (spiritual) family of God, and even those who are not! Those who ignore these responsibilities are worse than an "unbeliever" since many non-Christians care for their families and those unrelated within their communities.

Christians who want to put their faith into practice will appreciate how the early church, confronted with the challenges of persecution, division over doctrine, and ignorance of the faith, understood that Jesus' second greatest commandment to love others is unequivocally welded to loving God. Acts chapter 2 records the actions of these early believers as they relinquished their firm grasp on "property" and the love of it so that they might share *everything* they had for the benefit of those who had nothing. There lies what seems like the insurmountable challenge to the affluent American Christian society. The circumstances surrounding these Christians written about in the Book of Acts found many from the poorest class in the city of Jerusalem and even more from distant regions. They were not all from the same neighborhood and culture, nor did they all look or act the same. These early Christians understood and demonstrated social justice.

Christians are called to promote social justice wherever God places them and whenever injustice surfaces. One does not have to look very hard to find such opportunities, for there is never a shortage of injustice in our world (or our country). Social justice should be exercised with and among the various social classes of our society working towards equality and solidarity as we support economic egalitarianism and acknowledge the dignity and worth of every human being. This is not to suggest that the manufactured outcome of socialism or a cooperative economic organization is preferred, but that the injustices of society are eliminated so that access and opportunities are accessible. Social justice is an excellent means by which we can build bridges of reconciliation because it demonstrates in tangible ways our love, generosity, and concern by actively serving sacrificially.

Several times in this book I have referred to Faith Christian Fellowship, a church my wife and I would visit whenever we found ourselves in Baltimore. This church was one of the earliest inspirations for this book. If you have never experienced the power, harmony and love of a multicultural worship service, why not? You really don't know what you are missing. On the church's website, under the category labeled "mission/vision" you will find "Justice" defined as "Doing justice and loving mercy through crisis relief, community transformation through Christian community development (Ephesians 1:18-23, Ephesians 5: 13-17, Ephesians 6:5-9; Micah 6:8)."[22] Social justice cannot be addressed from the safe confines of your living room. Here is where the rolling up of sleeves and working alongside your brothers and sisters of color is needed. Here is where your action will meet your words and where new relationships will be formed through tangible acts of love. It is the demonstration of what we believe, communicating a desire for reconciliation without the necessity of words.

Amos was the prophet of justice. His passion was the plight of the helpless and poor while understanding that with the gift of privilege comes responsibility. In his words, Amos yearned for justice to come upon his nation like a tsunami. "But let justice roll on like a river, righteousness like a never-failing stream!" (Amos 5:24). The influential theological writer, John Stott, astutely notes, "In every sphere of society Amos saw evils that needed to be exposed. In the law courts magistrates trampled on the face of the poor, for justice had to be brought with bribes (v.12). In the marketplace merchants were guilty of 'skimping the measure' and 'boosting the price' (8:5). In upper-class mansions the wealthy were indulging in luxurious living, eating, and drinking, while ignoring the plight of the poor (4:1; 6:4-6). And in the sanctuaries worshippers were longing for the festivals to be over so that they could get back to their buying and selling (8:5)."[23] Sound familiar?

In his address to UNESCO concerning the role of culture in the life of nations, Pope John Paul II said, "We must ask how this common treasury of the human race, the treasury of so many different cultures, can be built up over time, and we must ask how best to respect the proper relationship between economics and culture without destroying this greater human good for the sake of profit, in deference to the overwhelming power of one-sided market forces. . .Man lives a really human life thanks to culture. . .Culture is a specific way of man's 'existing' and 'being'. . .Culture is that through which man, as man, becomes more man. . ."[24] It is interesting to note that these comments were received more enthusiastically by Third World countries than from Western Europe or the United States. That really comes as no surprise since most of the world's wealth has, traditionally, been centered in the West. The affluent West immediately feels threatened by any suggestion of our financial and moral responsibility, while those in the Third World view the Pope's comments through the "me" filter of need and hope. "Fundamental to the (American) spirit, then, is multiplicity and pluralism, not limitation and closure."[25] Redistribution should never be a forced implementation by government, but rather a willing and intentional gesture motivated by Christ's love for us and our love for others.

In an article on social justice for *USA Today,* Robbie Corey-Boulet discusses the growth of the Catholic Church in Africa, primarily a product of staying true to the tradition of justice for the poor. "In several African nations, half of the population is Catholic, and the church is perhaps the biggest non-government aid agency. Continent-wide, the church runs 55,000 schools and 20 universities that educate hundreds of thousands of Africans.

When some African leaders refused to acknowledge that AIDS existed in their countries, or refused to treat the disease, the Catholic missionaries and nuns moved through the most impoverished regions of the continent (providing) medical treatment and pastoral uplift."[26] Corey-Boulet goes on to say that the services offered at their schools and hospitals aren't just for Catholics, they are extended to all the population. It is this practical expression of one's faith that speaks louder than words; a message of love, unity, and acceptance through social justice.

Opportunities to improve one's lot exist in the United States unlike any other country in the world, which is one reason why it is truly a phenomenal nation. But to understand the challenges and limitations to these opportunities we must look upon them from a variety of perspectives. When our honest intentions are to comprehend more accurately how others perceive a scenario, our perspective will widen, enabling us to see the peripheral also. It takes deliberate and intentional actions which includes deliberation through honest conversation with those with whom we disagree.

THE DREADED "S" WORD

The topic of slavery has always been a lightning rod of division which is, obviously, avoided for a variety of reasons. American history is unlike any other county's history when it comes to the integration of various peoples through immigration (both legal and illegal) and slavery. The matter of ethnic relations from the minority's perspective is one that stems from patterns of ethnic discrimination imposed by the dominant white majority which has consistently held the power within society. Ethnic discrimination has always been a significant aspect of our history affecting our economics, domestic violence, and social policy.[27] European immigrants, Jews, Native Americans, Asians, Hispanics, and Middle Eastern immigrants have all experienced the compression of prejudice due to their ethnicity, religion or skin color, resulting in alienation from mainstream America and deliberate inopportunity. The African American assimilation differs from these other groups in that they are represented by a larger population, were brought to the United States unwillingly as slaves and that, due to their darker skin, can be immediately distinguished from the masses making it more difficult to "assimilate" into the existing society. The creation of Jim Crow laws made it nearly impossible for this group to improve their economic and social status following emancipation.

The man Job of the Old Testament came from a culture where slaves were held, most often as a result of military occupation, yet he understood the equality of humanity because he was a godly man. "If I have denied justice to any of my servants, whether male or female, when they had a grievance against me, what will I do when God confronts me? What will I answer when called to account? Did not he who made me in the womb make them? Did not the same one form us both within our mothers?" (Job 31:13-15). Job grasped the fact that we are all made in God's image and to view or treat a fellow creation with anything less than love and respect is to blatantly break the second greatest commandment, to "love your neighbor as yourself" (Mark 12:31). There are many parallels between slavery in the 19th century and segregation in the evangelical church in the 21st century. It's too easy to separate the two, but the premise remains the same. Any purposeful attitude and action embracing segregation due to the color of someone's skin or ethnicity is an attempt to demean the value of people, who are made in God's image, and misrepresents Christianity, and thus Christ.

As I write this our nation is celebrating the 126th birthday of the Statue of Liberty. The United States has always been the melting pot for the world's seekers, those looking for the opportunity to succeed under the protection of the shield of freedom. The Roman goddess of freedom stands in the New York harbor, broken chains at her feet. The UNESCO "Statement of Significance" describes the statue as a "masterpiece of the human spirit" that "endures as a highly potent symbol—inspiring contemplation, debate and protest—of ideals such as liberty, peace, human rights, abolition of slavery, democracy and opportunity."[28] The statue has been a beacon of freedom and equality that offered promise to millions seeking a better life for themselves and their families, but we must understand that this is the perspective mostly of lighter skin European and well-educated Asian immigrants. Unfortunately, it has not represented the same promise to all American citizens.

"The New Colossus" is a sonnet by Emma Lazarus (1849–1887), written in 1883 and engraved on a bronze plaque and mounted inside the lower level of the pedestal of the Statue of Liberty in 1903.

> The New Colossus
> Not like the brazen giant of Greek fame,
> With conquering limbs astride from land to land;
> Here at our sea-washed, sunset gates shall stand
> A mighty woman with a torch, whose flame
> Is the imprisoned lightning, and her name
> Mother of Exiles. From her beacon-hand

Glows world-wide welcome; her mild eyes command
The air-bridged harbor that twin cities frame.
"Keep, ancient lands, your storied pomp!" cries she
With silent lips. "Give me your tired, your poor,
Your huddled masses yearning to breathe free,
The wretched refuse of your teeming shore.
Send these, the homeless, tempest-tost to me,
I lift my lamp beside the golden door!"

A beautiful sonnet providing promise and a bright future for millions, but try to read this from a perspective of those deliberately oppressed. Shortly after the dedication, the Cleveland Gazette, an African American newspaper, suggested that the statue's torch not be lit until the United States became a free nation "in reality": "Liberty enlightening the world, indeed! The expression makes us sick. This government is a howling farce. It cannot, or rather does not, protect its citizens within its own borders. Shove the Bartholdi statue, torch and all, into the ocean until the 'liberty' of this country is such as to make it possible for an inoffensive and industrious colored man to earn a respectable living for himself and family, without being ku-kluxed, perhaps murdered, his daughter and wife outraged, and his property destroyed. The idea of the 'liberty' of this country 'enlightening the world,' or even Patagonia, is ridiculous in the extreme.[29]"

The white reaction to such a statement may initially be one of anger, viewing it as antagonistic from an unappreciative instigator. All of us view life through the tainted perspective of the "me" filter. How does this affect me? Am I being attacked and accused? It is only when we make an honest attempt to place ourselves in the position of the person expressing their thoughts that we begin to have some type of empathy, but it should be noted that we never truly appreciate the history of one man or a people because we do not have the same history. It should be from this starting point that we attempt to understand through compassionate eyes. Selfish anger must be placed aside and replaced with the realization and acceptance that there is, in fact, some truth to every accusation. The perspective of the person writing the editorial in the Cleveland Gazette is one that comes from anger stemming from oppression and mistreatment.

Imagine the prejudice, hatred and alienation the African American experienced in 1903. What is especially disheartening is the lack of social action taken by the white Christian community during the century and a half following emancipation.

In an address delivered in Cork, Ireland on October 23, 1845, Frederick Douglass talked about the hypocritical white Christian's stance on segregation (more specifically, slavery):

> "In no sound philosophy can slavery be justified. 'Tis at war with the best feelings of the human heart. 'Tis at war with Christianity. Wherever we find an individual justify[ing] slavery on such a pretext you will find him also justifying the slavery of any human beings on the earth. 'Tis the old argument on the part of tyrants. Tyrants have ever justified their tyranny by arguing on the inferiority of their victims. The Slavery of only part or portion of the human family, is a matter of interest to every member of the human family; slavery being the enemy of all mankind. I wish it distinctly to be understood that this is no feeling of merely intellectual interest, but 'tis also a matter of moral interest to you; since the morals it produces affect all men alike. I speak to Christian men and Christian women. The glory of Christianity is to be defended, to be maintained, but how, Mr. President, I ask, is Christianity to be defended and maintained if its professors—if those who stand forth as its advocates—are found with their hands dripping with the blood of their brethren? Why is Christianity to be maintained, if Christians stand by and see men, made in the image of God, considered as things—mere pieces of property?"[30]

How can a church perceive a man or woman as a person in need of God's saving grace, but still view them as not worthy to worship and commune with? Christianity can only evangelize the world by the loving actions of all who call themselves disciples of Christ and these expressions of love demand that we stand against oppression and hatred and demonstrate genuine care for others, especially those whose appearance is different than ours. There is no better place for this to start than in the American Evangelical church. Throughout world history we see numerous examples of how the church stood against evils and changed both the perception of the masses as well as government to bring about positive change. Consider the following poem written (and mailed) by B.T. Roberts, founder of the Free Methodist Church:

To my dear Sister,

The voice of a female slave
    "Am I not a woman and a sister"?

Though curly locks my head adorn
Though darkly sable be my face,
    Yet courses not within my veins
    The purple blood of Adam's race?

Though with the invader's ruthless hand,
From friends and home I'm torn away,
    To be a slave in Christian's land,
    Deprived of Freedom's genial ray;

Though Master's whip hath torn my back,
And made the crimson current flow,
    In torrents down my quivering flesh,
    Till Death had almost eased my wo;
Though Tyrant's galling chains enclose,
My mangled limbs in dire embrace,
    Though marks of bruises, and of blows,
    Eternity can ne'er efface;

Yet have I not that form divine
Which God to all mankind hath given?
    Is not that soul immortal mine
    Which e'er must dwell in hell or Heaven?

Abides there not within my breast
Devotion pure Affection deep?

Oppression's rod can ne'er arrest
Those powers of soul that never sleep.

As then if you were made a slave
You'd others have to feel for you,
Deeply within your heart engrave
For me such feeling deep and true.

Dear Sister keep the [*sic*] within as an amulet for the repulsion of that evil Spirit the Genius of Slavery.

Your affectionate brother
B.T. Roberts
Lodi March 20th 1845[31]

Sadly, as much as the church has done in standing up against societies' evils, there are at least as many examples of how the church has turned her back and ignored critical opportunities to stand in the face of oppression and, by doing and saying nothing, has allowed evil to prosper. Dietrich Bonhoeffer felt strongly that the German church was largely responsible for allowing the atrocities inflicted by the Nazis simply by remaining silent, as evident by the Declaration of Stuttgart.[32] The Declaration admitted that "Through us (the German Evangelical church), infinite suffering was brought over many peoples and countries" (parenthesis mine).[33] Wherever political ideology and majority agreement contradict biblical teaching, Christians *must* stand up, speak, and take action against it. Welcome persecution, my friend. The price is often high, and that is exactly why so few are willing to act upon the conviction of the Holy Spirit.

RESENTMENT FROM BOTH SIDES OF THE FENCE

Having interviewed numerous Christians of both black and white skin, I asked the obvious question of what they thought was the single biggest obstacle to reconciliation in the church. Whites state that blacks want them to pay for what their great, grandfather did. "Judge me for who I am, not for what my ancestors did." I hear the defensive phrase "sticking it to the white man" as an expression of anger, fear, and skepticism. If there be some truth to that assertion, those attitudes in themselves create division, but if we are to better understand our black brothers and sisters we must make an honest attempt to better understand their perspective that, like all of us, is painted by life experience. African Americans see less inclusivity in leadership and areas of power and decision-making as a major contributor.

Black resentment is a reality that creates additional challenges for both whites and blacks and hinders any clarity of perspective. Whites often feel as though resentment is unjustified and demonstrates a lack of appreciation for their efforts to reconcile and, in their opinion, blame individuals (or groups) by painting with a large condemning brush. This mentality, in turn, creates white resentment. They feel victimized themselves by having been placed in a "generalization box" that all whites are insensitive, lack understanding of the problem and are, overall, apathetic. It is a form of reverse-prejudice (which really makes no sense at all, because any bias is a prejudice. False assumptions create misconceptions and prevent a fair interaction based on the equality of a level playing field. In my opinion, there really is no such thing as "reverse-prejudice"). Some blacks respond with a "So how does it feel?" attitude of two wrongs make a right.

Both sides of the fence are guilty of "pigeon-holing." A pigeon hole is a very small hole made in a piece of wood for pigeons to enter and live in. This hole is only fractionally bigger than the pigeon itself, so the pigeon has little room to maneuver. To "pigeon hole" someone, is to stereotype a person by generalizations so that there is no room for movement by your self-created definitions of the person. I find myself constantly having to guard my heart from such assumptions and sinful opinions. We all do this. You've heard them all before: all White Anglo Saxon Protestants (WASPs) are a closed-group of wealthy suburbanites who are prejudiced. All African American young males are violent and hate-filled. All people who are on welfare are lazy and don't want to work. All fat people are undisciplined and lazy. And the list goes on and on.

As Christ-followers we must guard our tainted perceptions and be conscious of their innate nature of being severely flawed.

There has also been an appropriate sense of abandonment felt by the black community as white churches migrated from the inner city to the "safer" confines of suburbia. *Christianity Today* editor at large, Andy Crouch addresses the white exodus by observing that ". . .in many struggling urban neighborhoods the only functioning institutions are churches and liquor stores. To be sure, a certain number of churches left with their members to the suburbs two generations ago, and no one seized the suburban opportunity more vigorously than evangelicals.

But most black churches stayed put in their old neighborhoods even when many of their members had left. International arrivals started their own churches in neighborhoods (and buildings) other Christians had vacated. A whole generation of community development-oriented pioneers, inspired by Dr. John Perkins, planted roots in the toughest urban locations through the darkest days of the 1980s and 1990s."[34]

The lack of action (the demonstration of one's conviction) by white evangelicals is perhaps the greatest contributing factor fueling black resentment. Quoting the Breckenridges again, "Many (minorities) feel that the evangelical church has not actually 'entered into' suffering with them (parenthesis mine)"[35] This involvement requires participation and ongoing association. It involves grieving with the under-resourced and disenfranchised through genuine empathy. Empathy is only possible when you are involved in people's lives and begin to experience injustice through their eyes. Throwing money to the black community is an impersonal and passive way to keep one's distance while still appeasing one's conscience. As mentioned in the previous chapter, the "hit-and-run" effect of short-term missions in the inner city has little long-term impact when the reality is often "out of sight, out of mind," for those white folk offering their acts of service. We come back to our safe, sterile lives and refuse to be personally involved and committed to help change the world around us (especially if it's a few miles outside our immediate environment). Please do not take me wrong, I'm not saying that these efforts are devoid of any positive results for both the sending team and the receiving team. I'm not questioning the purity of their intentions, and yes, we do need more financial resources to accomplish long-term domestic mission goals, but this is only a beginning. Any thought of these efforts being a solution or having a lasting effect is simply shortsighted.

Bitterness is born from resentment. Paul tells us to "See to it that no one misses the grace of God and that *no bitter root* grows up to cause trouble and defile many" (Hebrews 12:15). Resentment is only possible where there is a lack of forgiveness and a warped sense of expectations, expecting little from yourself and much from others. It is a cancer which grows deep within the heart and smothers any flicker of love. It prevents Christians from becoming sanctified and transformed into Christ's likeness, and it makes our witness impotent to the world. Our African American brothers and sisters need to forgive their white siblings and the white Christian community must ask for forgiveness for their apathy and lack of love. The cure for resentment is the same for circumstantial depression, and that is to *serve and pray for others*. When we do that, we immediately take the focus off of ourselves and place the emphasis on others. This servanthood is rewarded with a genuine joy that comes from the Spirit. It builds up and edifies the Body rather than tears down and destroys. We are also rewarded with a new and godly perspective which, in itself, is an incredible blessing.

Perspectives are shaped by a variety of influences, not the least by both anger and ignorance, which are the primary culprits behind much of the slow progress toward reconciliation. A white friend of mine was an orphan by birth and when he was still quite young he was adopted by a loving black couple. His perspective was unlike many whites and blacks in this country. He grew up knowing he was different than his parents and siblings, yet the love and belonging he received from his family made the color-line insignificant; that is until the day Martin Luther King was assassinated. His elementary school was predominately black. Within minutes after the news of Dr. King's murder filled the streets, an African American teen walked up to my friend and punched him as hard as he could in the mouth. Both anger and ignorance were demonstrated from a perspective of seeing one's dream shattered. Despair, anger, and hatred stemmed from a perspective that James Earl Ray represented all whites, including my friend, and Martin Luther King represented all blacks. Little did the attacker know that my friend had more in common with him than he did with me. Violence, outrage, and controversy followed throughout the streets across the United States in a massive wave of riots. It's not that difficult to understand these perspectives.

Our perspective can only be godly when we exercise our faith through obedience. Peter tells us "Now that you have purified yourselves by obeying the truth so that you have sincere love for each other, love one another deeply, from the heart" (1 Peter 1:22). The Holy Spirit is the means by which we purify our hearts and this purification manifests itself by our active love for others. Luther adds, "For what end must we lead a chaste life? That we may thereby be saved? No: but for this; that we may serve our neighbor."[36] The characteristic of the church is its love (*Philadelphia*) toward their Christian brothers and sisters. That should always be the motive and perspective a Christian has toward a fellow believer. The way we then look at others is the way Christ viewed others, with great value and a heart committed to serve them.

ETHNIC INTERACTION IN BIBLICAL TIMES

In a world which was much smaller than it is today, I wondered what the perspective was towards those of color in biblical times. In the mysterious book of Song of Songs (Song of Solomon), biblical scholars have offered a variety of opinions as to the interpretation and purpose of this book of the Bible. An interesting verse is found in the first chapter. Verse 5 begins "Dark am I, yet lovely, O daughters of Jerusalem, dark like the tents of Kedar, like the tent curtains of Solomon. Do not stare at me because I am dark, because I am darkened by the sun." We know that Solomon had 700 wives and 300 concubines (1 Kings 11: 1-3), of which many were foreign women. A popular interpretation is that this woman's skin was dark (suntanned) from working in the fields and her darkened skin made her feel insecure. Certainly, this could be the case, however, she compares her skin to the "tents of Kedar" which were made of black goats' hair. I'm not sure the sun could darken a person's skin to that degree from working outside. She does not state that her face was darkened by the sun, but simply *she* was darkened by the sun. In any case, the lover, Solomon, is clearly taken by her and her darkened appearance did not sway his perspective in the least.

We also see in Numbers 12:1 that Moses married a Cushite woman. Cush proper is an area today which includes southern Egypt, Sudan and northern Ethiopia, and so, the people of Cush were dark-skinned. Some believe that this Cushite woman was the same woman mentioned as one of the seven daughters of Reuel/ Jethro, the Midianite priest or prince mentioned in Exodus (3:1, 4:18, 18:1-2 ff.) Whether or not Zipporah and the Cushite were different individuals is not important for our purposes. It suffices to know that Moses married a woman of dark skin from Africa. Ezekiel the Tragedian was a 2nd century Jewish dramatist whose only surviving work has been found, in fragments, in the writings of some of the early church fathers, including Eusebius and Clement of Alexandria. In this work, entitled Exagoge, Ezekiel the Tragedian states that Zipporah describes herself to Moses as a stranger in the land of Midian, and proceeds to describe the inhabitants of her ancestral lands in Africa:

"Stranger, this land is called Libya {an ancient name for the African continent}. It is inhabited by tribes of various peoples, Ethiopians, dark men. One man is the ruler of the land: he is both king and general. He rules the state, judges the people, and is priest. This man is my father {Jethro} and theirs."[37]

In Numbers chapter 12 we read that Moses's older siblings, Miriam and Aaron, rebelled and challenged his authority, seemingly because he had married a Cushite woman (v. 1). The exact reason for their criticism is not known, although it has been suggested that it stemmed from Miriam's jealousy, supported by verse 2, "'Has the Lord spoken only through Moses?" they asked. 'Hasn't he also spoken through us?'. . ." Yet, the rhetorical question "Can the Cushite change his skin?" in Jeremiah 13:23 suggests that the Cushites were people of a markedly different skin color from the Israelites, probably an African people. This is an excellent example of interaction between the different ethnic groups found in the Bible from which we might glean some wisdom. It is for you, the reader, to discern, with the help of the Holy Spirit, why God might have included specific language and details in His Word and what He wants us to learn from them. "All Scripture is God-breathed and is useful for teaching, rebuking, correcting and training in righteousness, so that the servant of God may be thoroughly equipped for every good work" (2 Timothy 3: 16-17).

Throughout the Scriptures we see people who were committed to fulfilling the greatest commandment were also the same people who loved their neighbor and understood that true discipleship comes through obedience to the will of God. In Acts 8 (vv. 26-40) we read the story of Philip's interaction with the Ethiopian eunuch. Philip's reaction was to *run toward* the Ethiopian and then later to travel with him. Philip was first guided by an angel (v.30) and then by the Holy Spirit (v. 29). It should not be overlooked that Philip was obedient to the prodding and direction of the Holy Spirit, something that all believers should heed. There is no indication whatsoever in this passage that Philip thought twice about beginning a relationship with this unknown man.

OUR PERSPECTIVE OF GOD

Someone else's perspective can seem completely alien to us, just as it did to me in a recent encounter. Not long ago I was in the fellowship hall of an African American church and saw a painting on the wall which caught my attention. When I moved closer I realized it was a picture of a black Jesus. I was taken back, to say the least! My first thoughts were that this was outrageous, possibly even blasphemous! Everyone knows that Jesus was a Middle-Eastern Jew; dark complexion maybe, but black? Of course, not! But, once my self-righteous anger subsided, I began thinking. . .okay, Jesus wasn't black-skinned, but what about God, his Father? Jesus' physical appearance reveals little if anything about how God looks physically, in fact, we are told that God is Spirit (John 1:18; 5:37; 6:46; 1 Tim. 6: 15-16). Yet, we are told that we (all humankind) have been made in the likeness of God. That raises a more complicated question. Is God dark-skinned or Caucasian? Does he have eyes like an Asian person? All those who have called upon the name of Jesus are God's *chosen people*. They are people with every skin color, every ethnicity and every varied physical appearance. The Apostle Paul explained that, just as the prophet Isaiah predicted, the Jews would reject Jesus as the Christ and so the offer of salvation would be extended to the Gentiles. It is through adoption that God becomes our Father, through Christ's atoning work on the cross, yet we are to inherit our Father's identifiable characteristics just as we do our earthly father's. The difference is that the characteristics we emulate from our Heavenly Father do not deteriorate and perish, like those we receive from our biological fathers.

It is important to remember that we were made in God's image. All humans, regardless of how they may look physically, are made to reflect characteristics of God Almighty! I don't know about you, but that truth blows my mind! While God is not confined to the physical limitations that humans are, we share in God's nature with com-municable attributes (personality, love, wisdom, holiness, justice). We are told that "Christ is the visible image of the invisible God . . . For God in all his fullness was pleased to live in Christ" (Colossians 1:15, 19). "The son reflects God's own glory, and everything about him represents God exactly . . ." (Hebrews 1:3).

Just as icons are intended to draw us closer to Christ, if that painting of the black Jesus brings people into a closer relationship with him, are we to be offended by it? Can we call the painting blas-phemous while we fail to see the blasphemous actions in our own lives? (Romans 2: 1-16). God created us in His own image while giving us a preview of Himself in His Son, Jesus Christ. "No one has ever seen God, but God the One and Only (Jesus Christ), who is at the Father's side, has made him known" (John 1:18 – parenthesis mine). No one has ever seen God in his essence, since God is Spirit; however, God took on visible/physical forms several times in the Old Testament to make Himself known to man (Genesis 32:30; Exodus 24:9-10; Judges 13:22; Isaiah 6:1; Daniel 7:9). The title that John gives Christ, "the One and Only," is perhaps a purposeful reiteration of verse 1 that "In the beginning was the Word, and the Word was with God, and the Word *was* God." The Word, of course, is Christ, the Son. Only in Jesus do we have a glimpse of God's essence.

NOTES:

CHAPTER 5: A PERSPECTIVE IN BLACK AND WHITE

[1]   Breckenridge, *What Color is Your God*, 12.

[2]   "Timothy C. Morgan , "Sailing into the Storm," *Christianity Today*, March 2012, 24.

[3]   Ibid.

[4]   Ibid., 27.

[5]   Tony Campolo, pastor, sociologist, author, and speaker, interview by author, 12 Feb. 2013, email held by author.

[6]   Rev. Stan Long , interview by author, 23 June 2012, recording held by author.

[7]   Rev. Craig Garriott, interview by author, 23 June 2012, recording held by author.

[8]   Tyrone A. Perkins, pastor of Westside Bible Baptist, interview by author, 26 Feb,2013, email held by author.

[9]   United States Conference of Catholic Bishops, "Brothers and Sisters to Us" doc. on-line]; available from http://www.usccb.org/issues-and-action/cultural-diversity/african-american/brothers-and-sisters-to-us.cfm; . accessed 22 Dec 2012.

[10]   Gary Martin, *The Phrase Finder* (2013) [database on-line]; available from http://www.phrases.org.uk/meanings/give-a-man-a-fish.html; accessed 11 Jan 2013..

[11]   Habitat for Humanity, "Habitat for Humanity fact sheet" doc. on-line]; available from http://www.habitat.org/how/factsheet.aspx; accessed 30 Dec 2012.

[12]   Critical Multicultural Pavilion, "The Undergirding Factor is POWER Toward an Understanding of Prejudice and Racism" [doc. on-line]; available from http://www.edchange.org/multicultural/papers/caleb/racism.html; accessed 15 Feb 2012.

[13]   Mark Galli, "A Most Personal Touch," *Christianity Today*, February 2012, 22.

[14]   Jacqueline Kirby, "Single-parent Families in Poverty" [doc. on-line]; available from http://www3.uakron.edu/schulze/401/readings/singleparfam.htm; accessed 1 Feb 2013.

[15]   Walter Brueggermann, The *Christian Century* (June 14, 2003) 30-31 [journal on-line]; available from www.christiancentury.org; accessed 23 Feb 2013.

[16]   Galli, *A Most Personal Touch*, 22.

[17]   Ibid.

[18]   Church "giving" includes more than tithing. We are to give all of ourselves for the work of Christ, including serving and actively exercising our spiritual gifts.

[19]   For our purposes, a giving unit is defined as a person, or group of people, representing one combined giver. For example, a family of four, where both the husband and wife work, would only be one unit. A single person would also be one giving unit.

[20]   Words of Mother Theresa, "Her Words" [doc. on-line]; available from http://www.ewtn.com/motherteresa/words.htm; accessed 11 Sept 2012.

[21]   Zacharias, *Has Christianity Failed You?*, 34.

[22]   Faith Christian Fellowship, "Mission/Vision" doc. on-line]; available from http://fcfchurch.org/mission-vision; accessed 20 May 2012.

[23]   John Stott, *Through the Bible – Through the Year"* (Grand Rapids: Baker Books, 2006), 81.

[24]   Pope John Paul II, *Memory and Identity*, (New York: Rizzoli, 2005), 84-85.

[25]   Ibid, 87. (It should be noted that Pope John Paul II was making this statement about Poland, not the United States).

[26]   Robbie Corey-Boulet, "Catholicism Thrives in Africa," *USA Today*, 13 March, 2013, 7A.

[27]   It should be noted that the non-profit organization "Free the Slaves" states that there are 27 million people in slavery all over the world. An outsider is drawn to ask what the motivations are to oppress another in such a way that their civil, or more accurately "God-given," rights of freedom and value are disregarded. Although hatred, prejudice and pride are all involved with the motivation behind slavery, without exception, it is always financial greed that feeds slavery. See http://www.freetheslaves.net/SSLPage.aspx. .

[28]   UNESCO, "Statue of Liberty" [doc. on-line]; available from http://whc.unesco.org/en/list/307; accessed 28 Dec 2012.

[29]   Wikipedia, "Statue of Liberty "[doc. on-line]; available from http://en.wikipedia.org/wiki/Statue_of_Liberty; accessed 5 Nov2012.

[30]   Frederick Douglass, "American Prejudice Against Color," An Address Delivered in Cork, Ireland, October 23, 1845 [database on-line]; available from http://www.yale.edu/glc/archive/1061.htm; accessed 9 Oct 2012.

[31]   Howard A. Snyder, *Populist Saints: B.T. and Ellen Roberts and the First Free Methodists* (Downers Grove: Eerdmans, 2006), 34-35.

[32] For more information on the confession of guilt that representatives of the Evangelical Church in Germany formulated in Stuttgart in September 1945, see http://www.ihr.org/jhr/v08/v08p-55_Lang.html.

[33] Ibid.

[34] Andy Crouch, "A New Kind of Urban Ministry," *Christianity Today,* November, 2011, 24.

[35] Breckenridge, *What Color is Your God*, 80.

[36] Thomas R. Schreiner, "1, 2 Peter, Jude," in *The New American Commentary* (Nashville, TN.: B & H Publishing, 2003).

[37] Wikipedia, "Cush (Bible)" Cush_(Bible) [doc. on-line]; available from http://en.wikipedia.org/wiki/; accessed 14 Jan 2013.

6

PICTURE THE POSSIBILITIES

Whether you turn to the right or to the left, your ears will hear a voice behind you, saying, "This is the way; walk in it." Isaiah 30:21

"'If you can'?" said Jesus. "Everything is possible for one who believes." Mark 9:23

I can do all this through him who gives me strength.
Philippians 4:13

*W*hat if? What would the possibilities be if the American Evangelical Church refused to accept the status quo and became united to end the ethnic division which has dominated itself for so very long? What could be accomplished? How would God bless the church if she decided to become obedient to her Groom and turn from her evil ways? Can you picture the transformation, not only in the church, but in people's lives? Can you stretch your mind to envision how it might even change *our nation?* We have stifled the work of the Holy Spirit in our churches for centuries. No wonder the American church is dying. The lost world has no appetite for what we are selling. But what if? What if we were to confess our sins of indifference, privilege, and disunity and turn from our ways? We have an Old Testament chock full of examples of how richly blessed people repented and turned to God. Why not us? Why not now? Why not dream of what can be. . .what should be?

A PREVIEW OF HEAVEN

Jesus reminded us that our hearts should long for our heavenly home even while we are sent into the world to share knowledge of Jesus Christ to all people and to make disciple-making disciples. When we have that correct perspective, our love will be reflected by the way we live our life here on earth. Our hearts, compelled with love for Christ, will manifest itself in the way we love others. ". . . . .For where your treasure is, there your heart will be also." Matthew 6:19-21. If we really want to change our world, we must begin with living an authentic Christian life, and that includes having a passion for unity within the church.

Heavenward! Have you ever wondered what heaven will look like? Certainly there will be many people there whom you did not expect to see and, by the same token, there will be even more who are noticeably absent. The church here on earth should be a reflection and preview of what heaven will look like. The local church should reflect the diversity of the community in which it stands and a (albeit, imperfect) representation of heaven, with many people of varying skin color and ethnicity singing, praising and worshiping our Lord and Savior in one unified voice. "Then a voice came from the throne, saying:

> Praise our God,
> all you his servants,
> you who fear him,
> both great and small!"

Then I heard what sounded like a great multitude, like the roar of rushing waters and like loud peals of thunder, shouting:

> "Hallelujah!
> For our Lord God Almighty reigns.
> Let us rejoice and be glad
> and give him glory!
> For the wedding of the Lamb has come,
> and his bride has made herself ready.
> Fine linen, bright and clean,
> was given her to wear."

Revelation 19: 5-8

Paul tells us in Philippians 3:20 that "our citizenship is in heaven," which is the motivation for the comments made by, Ralph P. Martin in his commentary. Quoting Dibelius, Martin writes, "We have our home in heaven, and here on earth we are a colony of heaven's citizens."[1] We can say that we have dual citizenship, one here on earth and one in heaven, the latter taking precedence. Why is it that we so easily forget that one is eternal, while the other is temporal? If we make all of our life decisions based on the eternal, rather than the temporal, we will be impacting people for the kingdom. If we live out our love in an all-inclusive, Christlike way, the Holy Spirit *will* accomplish things through us that cannot be fathomed. Our heart problem lies in our love for the temporal, those things that will one day end. Christian eschatology, as revealed in the Bible, offers a pretty clear picture of the end of this world and the promise of another. "Singing Billy" Walker reminds us:

> This world is not my home,
> I'm just a passing through,
> My treasures are laid up
> somewhere beyond the blue;
> The angels beckon me
> from heaven's open door,
> And I can't feel at home
> in this world anymore.
>
> William Walker, 1809-1875

If you are a disciple of Jesus Christ, you are not indigenous to this world, you are simply a spiritual tourist and as such, you are called to be an ambassador of your heavenly home. "Instead, they were longing for a better country—a heavenly one. Therefore God is not ashamed to be called their God, for he has prepared a city for them" Hebrews 11:16. Christians are sojourners and pilgrims (1 Peter 2:11-12). Both of these terms suggest that we are strangers who abide with those who are dissimilar and unlike us and that we are seeking a destination other than where we currently are on this earth. We are immigrating to heaven.

Some, however, have used this truth as an excuse for inactivity. Richard J. Mouw, influenced by the late Mennonite theologian John Howard Yoder, states in Christianity Today, "He convinced me that the most appropriate Old Testament models for political discipleship today are those folks who sought to be faithful to the Lord's will in pagan surroundings: Joseph administering justice in Pharaoh's courts, Daniel pleading the cause of the oppressed before

Nebuchadnezzar, Mordecai getting involved in a palace intrigue to save his people from destruction."[2] If Christians remain faithful to Christ's commands of unity, love, and discipleship, the church will impact a lost and heathen world, both politically and socially. We are not (positively) impacting our world because we are not living out the lives God has called us to. We don't truly believe either in God's promises or the commitment and responsibility of a disciple's life. We have not completely bought into the vision of what can be. . .what God *will* do in and through us when our faith becomes active, and not a license for complacency. We simply do not believe we can have much of an impact on a world enamored by sin and we most certainly have misunderstood the tremendous responsibility Jesus left us with when he commanded that we evangelize the world. For those of you who think that commandment was for the disciples, pastors and missionaries, you are very wrong. He was speaking to you, my dear friend. What would happen if we were to "seek first the kingdom of God?" We have forgotten that we are to be in the process of becoming transformed and sanctified into Christ's likeness, and that includes being a light in this world through our Christlike actions.

The prophecy of Daniel lays a foundation for the eschatological culmination in the Book of Revelation. Daniel had a vision of what is to come, an "everlasting kingdom" that will never be conquered. People from every corner of the earth, of every color and language group, will worship the Son of Man, Jesus Christ. "In my vision at night I looked, and there before me was one like a Son of Man, coming with the clouds of heaven. He approached the Ancient of Days and was led into his presence. He was given authority, glory and sovereign power; *all nations and peoples of every language* worshiped him. His dominion is an everlasting dominion that will not pass away, and his kingdom is one that will never be destroyed" (Daniel 7:13-14, emphasis mine).

Creating an all-inclusive society within the church, one that is representative of what heaven will look like, should be the goal of every local (visible) church. Christ's work at Calvary united Christians as the Apostle John expressed in his vision of the future; ". . .with your blood you purchased for God persons from every tribe and language and people and nation. You have made them to be a kingdom and priests to serve our God, and they will reign on the earth" (Revelation 5:9c-10). Many Christians have no idea what their spiritual identity is. We are a kingdom of priests! John goes on to echo what Daniel saw in his vision, the extensive ethnic representation of heaven. "After this I looked, and there before me was a great multitude that no one could count, from every nation, tribe, people and language, standing before the throne and before the Lamb. They were wearing white robes and were holding palm branches in their hands" (Revelation 7:9).

A LESSON FROM THE EARLY CHURCH

Multi-ethnic congregations understand that they are experiencing an authentic expression of faith. In the first century church we read where Jews and Gentiles worshipped together, but make no mistake, this was not without conflict. It is too easy for us contemporary Christians, two-thousand years removed from the dynamics that took place in the early church, to be oblivious to the tremendous challenges facing these early believers. If we look back to the Parable of the Good Samaritan we get a glimpse of the animosity Jews felt toward a group who were a mix of Jewish and Gentile ancestry (Luke 10:25-35). They despised the Samaritans, and it can be assumed that the feeling was mutual. Early Christianity was almost looked upon as a sect within Judaism, and one not very well received by the establishment. Even in Acts 11:19 we see that only Jews were being given the Good News of Jesus Christ, but as the apostles began to evangelize Gentile areas, divergence between believing Jew and Gentile surfaced.

As the church in Antioch grew there was internal bickering and division experienced by traditions and prejudice (Acts 15)[3], but the leadership *had a divine vision!* They looked at their goal, pressing "on toward the goal to win the prize for which God has called (them) heavenward in Christ Jesus" (Philippians 3:14), the "author and perfecter of our faith" (Hebrews 12:2). We share in this goal which includes the unity of the church as we grow in the faith and knowledge of Jesus Christ.

Merely tolerating plurality is not the same as lovingly approaching integration with excitement and anticipation of what God is going to do among us as a result of our heart-commitment to authentic worship and genuine unity. We need to take the initiative to achieve trans-ethnic understanding, making the effort to appreciate how others perceive things. Jesus always met people where there were. He always approached people from *their* unique situation, which is one reason why his ministry was so effective. The woman at the well accepted Jesus' criticism because she first felt his acceptance and love. The crowd that was incited to stone the woman caught in adultery was both convicted and humbled by Jesus' words so that their only possible response was to drop their stones and walk away. A little man, hated by all and known as the chief tax collector, climbs a sycamore tree to get a better look at this man named Jesus of Nazareth. Jesus invites himself to stay at Zacchaeus' house (which enraged the masses) but by meeting this man on his turf, Jesus' love resulted not only in Zacchaeus' repentance, but compelled him to make restitution to all he had swindled. When we meet people on their terms instead of ours, we build bridges. They see your actions and understand that you went the extra mile, and that type of selflessness has a profound effect on people. . .it moves people because it is so contrary to what they expect. Ending racism requires the church's role to witness to a lost world through its conscious responsibility manifested in reconciling action.

John the Baptist understood and identified the biggest obstacle for following Jesus obediently, that being SELF. Funny how some things never change. The same things that hindered spiritual growth two or three thousand years ago are the same things that hinder you and me today, for when it comes to our sin nature, humankind has not changed. Divisions within the church and the lack of desire to create harmony among people of various skin colors, is the result of selfishness. Self-seeking, self-pleasing, self-gratification are idols which put everyone else a distant second. As soon as we make ourselves and our desires more important than Jesus Christ, we get in trouble. That was John's premise when he proclaimed that "He (Jesus Christ) must become greater; I must become less" (John 3:30, parenthesis mine). Our selfishness is at the core of the lack of reconciliation among ethnic groups; however, both opportunity and challenges await us. Bruce Milne is spot on when he states: "Beginning from an ethnically and socially monotype base, the challenge is to move beyond the largely outmoded principle of congregation-building – 'people like us' – to courageously engage and embrace these 'different others' in Christ's name and create through the Holy Spirit 'diversity-in-unity churches, like the ones in the NT (New Testament) from Pentecost onwards. The blessings promise to be manifold, not least a larger Jesus Christ, and the possibility of becoming a congregational foretaste of the church's glorious future" (parenthesis mine).[4]

It is not merely an attitude or appeasement or even accommodation, rather it should be one of great anticipation and joy as we embrace other diverse "parts" of the body that has been lacking for too long. By acting in obedience to true unity we will benefit by experiencing perspectives, gifts, and blessings from spiritual relatives with whom we have yet to commune. It simply is not possible to experience these unique traits when we insist on associating with people who are clones of ourselves. Young people throughout history have often been the ones who have become dissatisfied with status quo. The youth are looking to us to see what we're going to do. For many young people, what they see is hypocrisy and it disgusts them. No wonder so many youth are fleeing the church. The biblical model for the health, growth and stability of the church is one of mentoring. It is imperative that the older men and women of the church exemplify the mentoring commands found in Titus chapter 2. Both older men (2:1) and women (2:4) are called to be teachers so that "the word of God may not be dishonored" (v. 5b NAS).

Younger adults have grown up in an American society which embraces multiculturalism and has resulted in less polarizing, while appreciating ethnic diversity. It is, most probably, easier for them to practice the expression of love for one's neighbor who looks differently from themselves, than it is the older generation. For some in the older group, having grown up in the racially turbulent 60s and early 70s, hostility and fear run deep. Some of these Christians (both white and black) harbor hatred and resentment which is kept locked in a dark closet deep within themselves. Yes, they would be embarrassed if the light exposed their filthy clandestine thoughts, but they refuse to confess this sin and deal with the issues and actions that nurture it. I am convinced that if older Christians in the church were to take their mentoring responsibilities seriously and model the loving, conciliatory interaction which God's word so clearly calls them to do, an ethnically-blended church more representative of heaven would be the result. The church is living with the ramifications and consequences of not adhering to the biblical pattern of the mentoring of the young by the spiritually mature.

Intervarsity took the lead several decades ago when it came to wanting, or more appropriately *needing,* a worship community which better represented the invisible, worldwide church. "The need to accommodate, honor and grow based on a recognition of diverse worship styles has never been more vital than in today's multicultural society and 'post-denominational' church. We all know that African-American and Hispanic and Asian and Anglo approaches to worship are uniquely their own."[5] Intervarsity took the initiative on multicultural worship because they saw that no one in the country was acting on what the established church was ignoring. College students began to be dissatisfied with the segregation of churches and had a sense that this is not how church should be. Campuses began stressing that realization more and more in the 1990's. And the young shall teach the old.

MY CHRISTIAN-SOCIAL EVOLUTION

I would be remiss if I didn't share the metamorphosis that happened in my life, specifically when it came to my sinful attitudes and actions toward people of color. My Christian-social evolution is a result of the power of the Holy Spirit who radically changes the hearts, minds, and attitudes of men. The Holy Spirit is in the business of changing hearts. That is what He does, and He does it well! Unfortunately, many American Christians are not being transformed into the likeness of Jesus Christ (2 Cor. 3:18) simply because they are thwarting the work of the Holy Spirit (Acts 7:51). If Christians looked and acted more like Jesus, we'd have less difficulty in incorporating and embracing ethnic unity. There is a yielding of the heart which is prerequisite for being transformed into Jesus' likeness and that demands complete surrender on our part. Those who have placed their faith and trust in Jesus Christ and have received God's saving grace have had to succumb to the prodding of the Holy Spirit in surrendering control over their own lives, but this is not a "once-and-done" action. Just as we must preach the Gospel to ourselves *every day*, we must also surrender our will *every day* in order to hear God's voice. When we fail to surrender our will to the leading of the Spirit, we fall prey to the power of the flesh and *too easily* yield to its sinful desires.

The reason I am convinced that the Holy Spirit changes lives is because I have experienced it firsthand. He has turned my life completely around, 180 degrees. He changes perceptions and biases, I am proof of that. Having learned bigotry through community influences, I developed preconceived opinions based on ignorance and false information at a young age. Being small for my age and a late-bloomer (I grew 3 inches and gained 25 pounds once in the military), I was on the losing end of too many fist fights, and even though these fights were with boys of white skin as well as black, my suspicion of anyone of color grew. I developed a vehement hatred for most all people, but those of color headed the list. My sweeping generalization created a rationale that all African Americans were violent people (interestingly, I gave a pass to the white community even though a fair amount of my fist fights were with white youths!). My life philosophy and ideology were based on hatred and igno-rance. Failing to recognize that few occupational and educational opportunities often translates into unemployment and poverty; I developed a philosophy that black unemployment was simply the result of laziness and a parasitic mentality. In retrospect, my preju-dice was fueled by ignorance, fear, and a self-created isolation from all people of color by refusing to enter into any meaningful dialogue or interaction with anyone that wasn't white. I had not yet entered into a personal relationship with Jesus Christ and so, without the guidance of the Holy Spirit, I was stumbling along in an attempt to develop my own philosophy of life.

Today it is commonplace for police to be stationed at schools across the country, especially in urban areas. However, when I attended high school in the early 1970s this was not common practice, yet there were police officers stationed on every floor of our school to prevent racial violence. Everyday events were influenced by the atmosphere of violence, hatred, and fear. Which route you would walk home, where you would hang-out on the weekends, what ball field you would play at, were all dependent upon the color of the attendants. That's just the way it was. At school it was common practice to crack the door to the boy's bathroom and, if it was populated with white boys, you entered; if it was black, you held it in! If you were African American, you didn't dare enter the bathroom that had no blacks in there or you would be beaten to a bloody pulp! The same rules applied if you were white skinned and tried to enter a bathroom dominated by blacks. But as I was developing my personality of a hateful isolationist, God had other plans for me. Although I didn't know it at the time, I was desperately seeking for the love, acceptance and fulfillment that only Jesus Christ could offer. My exhausting attempts to fill the "God hole" were becoming disastrous and futile, but little did I know that I was being led toward a series of interacting, relational opportunities that would (albeit, slowly) chisel away at my self-made wall of prejudice built with blocks of hatred.

By the time the summer of my 16th birthday arrived, my parents were at their wits end. Having had three children who were compliant, obedient, and good students, my parents couldn't believe their fourth child could be so different. Rebellious, violent, unfocused, and a horrible student, I caused one family emergency after another. In the vein of the "Scared Straight" television show (where troubled youths are taken to a prison where inmates terrify the teens by showing what the future holds for them should they not change their ways), my parents shipped me off to a friend's tobacco farm in Lynchburg, South Carolina. There I spent the summer topping tobacco along with 20 or so African American farmhands. Topping tobacco is the process of manually breaking off the flowering stems and/or the "suckers" which steal nourishment from the valuable tobacco leaves. If topping isn't done, the plants become reproductive seed producing plants instead of a leaf producing cash crop.

I, along with the African Americans, would head out to the tobacco fields early in the morning under the unbearable Carolina sun, taking occasional 5 minute breaks to drink cool water from the ladle whenever the horse-drawn wagon would appear. Drinking from the same ladle that African Americans used was no small feat for the angry young man from north of the Mason-Dixon Line, but working all day with a parched throat in the summer heat without hydration was a much worse alternative. I was acutely aware of my surroundings and although I kept to myself and had little to say to my African American co-workers, they treated me with kindness and respect.

The first day of work provided many a life-lesson, not the least was the arrangement for dinnertime. Coming from Pennsylvania, I didn't realize that the big meal of the day in the south was at noon, and that meal was called dinner (supper was the evening meal). The farmer came with the wagon at noon and all of the workers would jump on the back of it and head for the farmhouse. The farmer's elderly mother and a large black woman had prepared a culinary feast! Fried chicken, corn bread, collard greens, potato salad, blackeyed peas, fried okra, lemonade and grape Nehi soda filled the picnic table. Soaking wet from sweat, I quickly grabbed a seat along with the other workers, more than ready to devour an entire bird by myself! Just when we were about ready to dig-in, the farmer's mother, a nasty old bird herself, opened the screen door and yelled "Glenn, you come on in here. You'll be eating with us." Now, prejudiced or not, I knew it wouldn't be a good thing to eat in the cool comfort of the white farmer's dining room when my fellow farm hands were experiencing fellowship under the shade of the big poplar tree. I declined the old woman's offer. The expression on her face was both shock and anger. An old black farm hand grabbed me gently by the shoulder and said, "Now you go on in there, boy. It's alright." A bit naive, I was appalled that they would segregate the work crew and place me in a precarious position between the two parties. That afternoon back in the fields I couldn't help but feel the injustice and bigotry toward the black workers. This was just the beginning of God's plan to soften my calloused heart.

I entered the Navy at age 17. Young and impressionable, I found myself in an environment of forced conformity which dictates teamwork. A military ship is an interesting microcosm of society, minus the female species (at least when I was serving, in the 70's). It was a potpourri of socio-economic backgrounds, education, religious beliefs, personalities and ethnicity which made up this floating mini-city. What you quickly learn is that *everyone* is dependent upon each other. Although I was trained in Electronic Warfare (Soviet intelligence/electronic countermeasures), I, along with ever other sailor, had to be well-trained in shipboard "damage control." Damage control is an emergency control process in which shipmates are assigned responsibilities during situations that may cause the sinking of a ship (like being hit with a torpedo). Should our ship ever be struck by enemy fire causing a hole in the skin of the ship, whoever is in that work space would be required to act swiftly to stop the leak and minimize any damage. Every man aboard had been trained in damage control. A ship does not have the luxury of having a surplus of resources. Everyone is dependent upon each other. Living with 300 other men on a 322 foot guided-missile destroyer in the middle of the ocean strongly encourages you to get along with the other shipmates! Slowly I began to form friendships with a few African-American and Filipino shipmates.

After the navy I attended Temple University, located in the predominately black section of North Philadelphia. Temple takes pride in the fact that it is the most ethnically diverse university in America. A few friendships were formed with people of color and dialogue and mutual respect took root. Here again, God led me to a place where interaction with people who looked differently than me was inevitable and many of the challenges I faced were shared by my diverse colleagues.

Soon after my children were born, I moved my family to an affluent white suburb of Philadelphia. When my son first began playing baseball in little league, I'll never forget my experience sitting in the stands that very first game. Several white fathers welcomed me and, after asking what I did for a living, inquired about what country club I belonged to. I told them I didn't belong to any club which led them to ask if I even played golf. I did. Of course, they told me they could get me into one of their country clubs and possibly have the required (sizable) bond waived. When I thanked them but declined their offer they were stunned! It was inconceivable to them that, if I played golf, I would not join one of the local clubs. This is how they were defined as men. This was their "boys club," exclusively white and a place where the women wouldn't bother us. A place where "men can be men." It was one of those times in my life when I felt like a round peg in a square hole. I looked over the stands and saw an African-American father sitting by himself. I quickly formed a relationship with him finding that I had more in common with him than I did with any of the white guys! Neil and I remain close friends to this day. This was all part of a much bigger plan of God's.

After college I worked in sales for several flexible packaging companies which required that I travel all over the country and meet with a variety of different people. God wouldn't give up on me. After years of running from God and his most incredibly gracious offer of eternal life and a personal relationship with him though his Son, I surrendered my life to Christ. He was determined to mold me into something very different than what I had become prior to surrendering my life to Christ. All of those life experiences were used by God to soften my heart, convict me of my sin of hatred, and create a passionate heart for true ethnic reconciliation in America's churches.

My enlightenment journey reached a climax when God led me to attend the Philadelphia campus of Bethel Seminary of the East. I thank God for the ethnically diverse student body and the truly loving environment that Bethel provided as well as the many wonderful relationships which were formed. I was mentored by Tyrone Perkins, an African-American professor and pastor and it didn't take long before we quickly became good friends as we found that we needed to become transparent and vulnerable with each other if any meaningful spiritual formation was going to take place.

When I was completing my seminary studies I felt led by the Holy Spirit to pursue ordination. I was attending a Presbyterian church in rural northeast Pennsylvania at that time, which normally would not be a problem, but since I was attending a Baptist seminary, the Presbytery would not allow me to become ordained in the Presbyterian faith. I had to find a Baptist church that would adopt me and support me in my ordination. I asked my mentor, Tyrone Perkins, if his church would consider becoming my sponsoring church knowing quite well that this might be a bit out of their comfort zone, but after interviewing me they graciously accepted me with open arms and welcomed me as one of their own. I praise God for Westside Bible Baptist Church and their influence in my life!

It has been said that if you want to discern who your closest six friends are, or those whom you most admire and respect, think about what six persons you would want to be the pall bearers at your funeral. The metamorphosis of my life has brought me to a place where half of my pall bearers will be African American. From a place of hatred and prejudice to a place of inclusivity is only possible through the power of the Holy Spirit! Deep within me I understand that my hatred of those of color was a reflection of my hatred for myself. True freedom would never be within reach as long as I willingly chained myself to the bondage of hate. To be an agreeable participant to hatred is to loathe oneself, for deep within our core, deep within our heart, we have an understanding of our inseparable connection to the universal brotherhood of all humankind, no matter how suppressed that knowledge is. I am so very humbled and grateful for the wonderful journey on which the Holy Spirit has taken me.

I'm not the only person who has a story of incredible metamorphosis. I have seen this change happen in people over and over again. In his thorough commentary on the Gospel of Matthew, Michael Wilkins shares the story of his friend, Tom Tarrants who was a former Ku Klux Klan member during the turbulent 1960s and 1970s. "The transformation of his life is miraculous, as his hatred was replaced by love, and his bigotry with reconciliation. Together with John Perkins, a former black activist, they have written a book entitled *He's My Brother,*[6] which not only tells their stories but also presents a workable strategy for building bridges of understanding and reconciliation between peoples of differing backgrounds and color."[7]

THE CONCEPT OF PEACE

Concept is an idea formed from inference. Inference is the act or process of deriving logical conclusions from premises known or assumed to be true. We know that in God there is truth. We also know that God loves peacemaking. The only possible reason why a Christian would not seek peace would be that their heart is spiritually ill. Make no mistake, it is the heart that controls the mind (Matthew 12:34; Mark 7:21-23). Real change is possible only if our hearts are right with God and it is time for many of us to stop ignoring our condition and to spend some serious time in solitude, listening to what the Holy Spirit has to reveal to us. This disclosure by the Holy Spirit is bound to bring conviction and expose those heart-attitudes which have caused our sanctification to become lethargic. Many of us fill our days to the brim, with anything and everything to prevent any possibility of a "quiet time." Many of us fall to sleep with the television or stereo on, or with pharmaceutical aids to numb us to sleep. . .anything to distract us from the silence where we may hear the soft voice of God whispering to us. Solitude is the vehicle by which we are most often spoken to, and it is in this unobtrusiveness that we can hear God's voice. Here is where conviction often comes. I see a connection between solitude and conviction; meditation and revelation.

Search your heart. "Search me, God, and know my heart; test me and know my anxious thoughts. See if there is any offensive way in me, and lead me in the way everlasting" (Psalm 139: 23-24). David, a man after God's own heart constantly searched his heart. He knew that in the corners of his heart he would find sinful dirt that was swept under the rugs and he desperately wanted God to reveal those sins to him so that he could take the necessary action to execute those dangerous sins. We must do the same and have our motives exposed! If we create a situation to be with someone of color simply so that we can be seen as a contemporary, accepting, politically correct and a "nice" person, we are doing it for the wrong reason and our efforts are worthless. Search your heart. Evaluate your motives. When we fail to pursue Christlike peace with others, we fail at the second greatest commandment and misrepresent Christ to a desperate world.

There is a growing attraction by seekers toward the peace-loving message of many New Age religions. It is a welcoming environment for all who are seeking an answer to the meaning of life. It should be heartbreaking to all Christians that these false religions, filled with deception, are more inviting and accepting of people from all walks of life than many of our evangelical, Bible-preaching churches.

Recently I was driving on the Atlantic City Expressway when a billboard from the Baha'i Faith caught my eye. It simply read that they were a religion that seeks universal peace. I found an explanation of these faith-based principles in excerpts from the public talks of 'Abdu'l-Bahá in America in 1912, published in The Promulgation of Universal Peace. "'A fundamental teaching of Bahá'u'lláh is the oneness of the world of humanity. Addressing mankind He says, 'Ye are all leaves of one tree and the fruits of one branch.' By this it is meant that the world of humanity is like a tree, the nations or peoples are the different limbs or branches of that tree and the individual human creatures are as the fruits and blossoms thereof.'"[8] This sounds eerily familiar to Jesus' teachings that He is "the Vine and we are the branches. Apart from Christ, we can do nothing" (John 15:5). Again we see that the Great Deceiver, Satan, disguises himself as a messenger of peace. Why is it that the lost world can often propagate peace better than we Christians have?

John Lennon's "Imagine," is a song of harmony and unity to many and is still frequently played on the radio due to its popularity. The song asks us to ponder,

Imagine all the people living life in peace. . .

You, you may say
I'm a dreamer, but I'm not the only one.
I hope someday you'll join us,
And the world will be as one

Imagine no possessions.
I wonder if you can.
No need for greed or hunger,
A brotherhood of man.
Imagine all the people sharing all the world.

What Mr. Lennon failed to realize was that his imagined utopia is impossible and unobtainable without the sacrificial work of Jesus

Christ empowered by the Holy Spirit. It's simply a contradiction. He would like a world without heaven, hell or "religion," in other words, no God. It is true that "religion" has done much to dishonor the name of Jesus Christ, killing masses of people all in the name of righteousness, but Jesus never preached a message of religion. In our own power, the vision of unity and ethnic harmony is a dead impossibility. The dream of everyone "living for today" is realized in the here and now, and that is part of the problem. Our society is living for today and it has resulted in hate, violence and apathetic indifference. A life of self-gratification and no consequences is a world of denial and hopelessness. The church has an incredible opportunity to be a witness to what the power of Christ can do for a world filled with abhorrent selfishness.

GOD'S CREATIVITY

I never grow old at the wonder of experiencing God's handiwork through his creation. His unfathomable creativity never ceases to blow my mind and without doubt it is one of his greatest attributes. That is why my wife and I moved from the urban/suburban America to the mountains of northeast Pennsylvania. There, everyday, we are recipients of a fantastic show by a multitude of birds, deer, fox, bobcats, bear, porcupines, eagles and a variety of other wildlife. Throughout the animal kingdom God's magnificent power and creativity is demonstrated and when we experience his handiwork, a Christian's heart naturally turns to praise and worship (Psalm 19; Isaiah 65:17-25; Romans 8:18-25). The Swedish poet Carl Gustav Boberg articulates well the prodigious supremacy of our Lord and Savior, the author of all creation (Colossians1:16; John 1:3; Hebrews 1:2):

How Great Thou Art (Second Stanza)

When through the woods and forest glades I wander
And hear the birds sing sweetly in the trees;
When I look down from lofty mountain grandeur
And hear the brook and feel the gentle breeze;

Then sings my soul, my Saviour God to Thee; How great Thou art!

How great Thou art! Then sings my soul, my Saviour God to Thee;

How great Thou art! How great Thou art![9]

One of the fascinating features of our Lord's inspirational work is that he did not make one bird, but rather over 10,000 species of birds; from the ostrich to the hummingbird (talk about creativity!). He made 300,000 species of beetles! God loves variety! He made mammals like the elephant which weigh over 15,000 pounds, animals that almost look silly, like the duck-billed platypus, and animals that can be domesticated for our enjoyment, like dogs and cats. God could have made the entire earth to be viewed in shades of black, gray and white, like the way we used to watch television in the "olden" days, but he didn't. He painted his creation with an infinite amount of colors from his palate for our enjoyment.

Isn't it wonderful that God didn't make all the animals to look exactly the same? Isn't it wonderful that *we* don't all look the same? Believe me, I don't want a world full of people who look just like me, do you? Let us celebrate the fact that we do not all look the same, that we are not simply clones of each other! The challenge is not to reject or extinguish one's cultural heritage or to "make-believe" that we don't see the color of someone's skin (which is impossible to do), but to accept with love and marvel at the diversity of God's creation seen in fellow human beings whose skin has been painted with the beautiful hue by God's artistic hand.

The theme throughout the early church was always diversity within unity. When was it that we dropped the ball? We *can* change the erroneous direction in which the church has been heading. We *can* stop divisive judging and sinful indifference towards our brothers and sisters of color. The question that Paul asked the Roman church can be asked of us. "But you, why do you judge your brother? Or you again, why do you regard your brother with contempt?" (Romans 14:10a).

I've always found it curious how people have a tendency to reject anyone who does not look like them, yet most everyone seems to work hard, and spend hundreds if not thousands of dollars, to look more like people who are different than themselves. Sounds like a contradiction, doesn't it? People with straight hair get perms so that they'll have curly hair. People with wavy or curly hair often get their hair straightened. People who have light skin tan themselves, and if the outside temperature doesn't allow them to lie outside, they pay money to lie on tanning beds or go into tanning booths to become darker!

You are uniquely made (Psalm 139: 13-18). Be yourself while embracing those who don't look anything like you. We *are* different, and that's more than okay, that is wonderful! God's creative world is full of diversity, so it would make sense that he would make people quite different from each other *on the outside*. But our inner beings are very similar. Abraham Maslow's hierarchy of needs expressed in his 1954 book *Motivation and Personality* outlines the pattern through which human motivations normally move. The categories include Physiological, Safety, Belongingness and Love, Esteem, and Self-Actualization.[10] These groupings include basic needs that must be met before the desire for less essential needs. All people share the need for these stimuli. None of this should come as a surprise to Christians, because they look to Christ for those needs. The most surprising thing about those people who are prejudiced toward people whose skin is different than their own is that we are much more alike with these people than we are different. The differences should be insignificant to a Christian. Stereotypical opinions of people keep us from some of the most beautiful relationships that God intended for us to have.

THE LOCAL CHURCH

The home is an intimate setting. This is our safe haven, which is exactly why it is a very warm and friendly gesture to open your doors to others. What if you were to invite people of color into your home? What about going to their homes? How would that initiate new relationships? One of the successes in today's evangelical church has been the development of small groups, often called satellite groups or "home churches." This is a return to the early church format seen in The Book of Acts. One of the reasons these groups met at people's homes was out of necessity due to the persecution believers experienced in large group gatherings. Today, people are meeting during the week for Bible study and are receiving both social stimulation and a developed closeness by sharing burdens and praying for each other. It is in this environment that people feel safe and even vulnerable. The "Lone Ranger" syndrome is a myth which tells the lie that you are the only Christian with problems, or the only one who struggles with the spiritual journey or some sin in your life. We're told that if we only had more faith or believed a bit more that we wouldn't have these problems. The real crime is that we begin to believe that everyone else in the church is holy and righteous and don't have problems with their marriage, or children, or finances, or our faith. It's all a lie, but it can easily get our attention when we only worship in a large group setting for one hour on Sunday morning. Small groups provide a sense of community and it is the model of discipleship found in God's Word. If we would purposely seek people of color to be included in these small group Bible studies, I am convinced many sinful walls would begin to crumble. In fact, it would be nearly impossible not to build meaningful relationships with each other. Prayer is an intensely intimate act in which we share each other's burdens. How can we humbly approach our Creator and have anything but love for our brother and sister in Christ praying alongside us?

Addressing culture and community, the Breckenridges make an observation which reminds us of the need to be sensitive to the "newcomer" that enters our established group setting. "The Christian response to multiculturalism calls us to an affirmation of the personal worth of each person in our society." [11] Unless we view this person as an equal, created, just like us, in the image of God, our reaction will be counterfeit. They continue by explaining that "Such affirmation means entering into a meaningful relationship with all who enter our midst. The attempt to create such community will require churches to address challenges which relate especially to multiculturalism, specifically *stranger anxiety* and *ethnic identity*."[12]

We need to be bold in trying new and creative ways to accomplish ethnic unity in the American church, and sometimes that calls for radical, deliberate church integration. What would happen if we stepped out in faith and took half of the congregation of an African-American church and "changed places" with half the congregation of a white church? Radical, yes, but we need drastic and sweeping change in our evangelical society! Partnership with other churches, especially if your church's surrounding community is "mono-cultural." This intentional bridge-building will create acculturation, a change in the cultural behavior and thinking through meaningful interaction with another culture. Rather than viewing contributions from an "outsider" as a threat to your church's "comfortable" style of worship, view this visitor as a gift from God bringing fresh and exciting ways to worship, perhaps adding some variety to what very well may have become a stagnant, repetitious ritual, rather than a heart-felt expression of love, worship and gratitude to our Lord and Savior.

S.D. Gaede speaks of the "natural" inclination for American Christians to want to gravitate toward people of likeness. He states:

> "American Christians have the tendency to worship with those who are like them – ethnically, economically, and so on. If we approach community along those same stratified lines and our "socializing institutions" turn out to be white and middle-class, then our communities will not represent the body of Christ; they will not have all the insights and gifts of the body; and we will not wind up teaching the whole, life-changing truth of Scripture."[13]

Worship styles are just that, a "style," a preference. There's nothing wrong with preferring a specific worship style, what is wrong is when we put the emphasis on the *style* of worship rather than the *intent* and *focus* of our worship (as if one style is more spiritual than another). The purpose of the church is to worship God (Luke 4:8; John 4:23; Rev. 4:10), and we are to do so in unity with love. When the body has problems with unity, the body has problems with sin. When we are determined to force our style of worship on others our perspective is warped and motives sinful. If the truth be known, I seldom enjoy all of the songs sung in the worship services

I have attended. Specifically, the melodies sometimes disagree with me, but *it is not about me or my preferences!* When I don't care for a specific tune the congregation is singing, I simply pay more attention to the lyrics – the *words* of praise! Even if the song may not be a favorite of mine, I am often edified and praise-filled when I see my brothers and sisters in Christ glorifying and praising our Triune God.

WHO IS TO BLAME?

Who really is to blame for the American Evangelical refusal to exemplify Christlike unity and ethnic reconciliation? We can certainly blame past generations for their apathy and lack of action, but then the question is, why haven't *we* done anything about it? Is it our church leaders fault? Our pastors? Does the problem fall solely on the white community? Do other ethnic congregations take some of the blame? The truth is that *any* and *all* Christians who refuse to love true unity and who refuse to influence those who oppose such unity are guilty of the state of the American church. It is your problem. It is my problem.

Shame on you pastors who refuse to take creative steps and deliberate action to build ethnic bridges and shame on you for not making it a priority in your church. . .for fearing more about your congregation's reaction and your job security than about being obedient to your Heavenly Father and pleasing *him*. Some of you are more concerned with getting more convert notches in your belt than you are with obedience to unity, ethnic reconciliation, and social justice. You think you are winning souls for Christ when your hypocrisy is turning untold numbers away from the faith. Jesus had some strong words for the Pharisees who were doing something similar. "Woe to you, scribes and Pharisees, hypocrites, because you devour widows' houses, and for a pretense you make long prayers; therefore you will receive greater condemnation. Woe to you, scribes and Pharisees, hypocrites, because you travel around on sea and land to make one proselyte (convert); and when he becomes one, you make him twice as much a son of hell as yourselves (parenthesis mine, Matthew 23:14-15). Craig Blomberg observes that "The language here is strong ('son of hell') but accurate for any not following the way of the true and living God. Sometimes shock treatment is needed, especially, and primarily, for wayward religious leaders professing the truth."[14]

Shame on you wealthy business men and women who hoard your precious wealth, refusing to share ridiculously and abundantly with the many in need. How quickly you have forgotten where it is that you should store your treasures (Matthew 6:19-20). You are the same people who have done nothing to help build bridges, even though you have the resources, often because of the sacrifices required. Yes, these symbolic bridges cost money, they are not free. In many cases it is a lack of resources which has squelched dreams and plans for constructing these bridges of reconciliation. Your refusal to adopt a lifestyle of sacrificial giving is an embarrassment to the church and destroys your Christian witness. Shame on you as you demur any attempt to leave your ivory palaces and well-manicured lawns and venture into neighborhoods in need so you can establish new relationships and recognize the needs of others.

Shame on you African Americans and other ethnic groups who instead of building relationships with whites, build walls of isolation and assume that whites need to take the initiative for developing dialogue and meaningful relationships. Shame on those of you who have refused to offer forgiveness to the white community, instead holding on to grudges and bitterness. Shame on all you Christians who think that when someone of a different color extends the right hand of fellowship that they automatically have an ulterior motive, assuming that the gesture could not simply be an act of friendship, kindness, and love. Shame on all Christians whose heart is stained by prejudice while force-fitting others into insulting, pre-conceived and demeaning categories. You have made a mockery of Jesus Christ and the faith.

When we reject our spiritual brothers and sisters, we reject Christ. It is much more than indifference or neutrality; it is a deliberate discarding of a person's value. Rejection is one of the greatest pains in the human experience. It causes self-doubt and raises a question of one's worthiness. It makes the body of Christ incomplete and lacking, causing the church to function without all of its intended parts. Alienation of others is a choice which distances one from the unity and interdependency intended by our Creator. Mercy and love annuls alienation.

YOU AND ME

Instead of waiting for some "great" man or woman to miraculously mend the fabric of ethnic relations in our country, we must assume the responsibility and come to the realization that spiritual revival and ethnic reconciliation begins with you and me! Never underestimate the power of one person's boldness empowered by the Holy Spirit. The stirring of people's consciousness with a message of truth and life is a contagious product which will have a far-reaching and significant impact on the American Evangelical church. The American Evangelical church is moving glacially towards resolving its deep-seated problems of unity and reconciliation. It is ripe for a revival of prodigious proportion. The time is right; the time is now! With the empowering of the Holy Spirit, *you* can change our world and *you* have a much greater influence on others than you may know. Stop waiting for someone else to step up to the challenge, for as you step out in faith, knowing that what you are doing is a reflection of your love and trust in Jesus Christ, others will follow! The church groans for the reconciliation which has escaped us for too long. *Let us be the generation that corrects this age-old crime against Christ's people.*

Recently there have been a series of television commercials for an insurance company where a person's "good acts" are seen by others and has a contagious domino effect. A man drops his briefcase while running to catch a bus and a young woman, at the risk of missing her bus, stops and helps the man pick up his loose papers. That is seen by a young man and when he's at work and sees spilled coffee on the break room floor; he stops and cleans it up. That is seen by someone else and they are motivated to react selflessly when an opportunity arises, and so on and so on. The tag line is "Everyday millions of people choose to do the right thing." The connotation is that doing something kind, doing the right thing, can have contagiously positive effects on all of society. I know. . . if it was only that easy, but what if the church was to set such an example for the world to emulate. . .consistently? What if the church helped form significant interethnic relationships, built on Jesus' all-inclusive love? These people within the church are the same people who go out into the world every day; to their jobs, to their children's activities, and by living a life that demonstrates unconditional love for everyone, including people who are of another culture or ethnicity, the world will stand up and take notice. Picture the possibilities! The affirming domino effect on society is obvious. Ultimately, the objective is to be obedient to our Heavenly Father by being disciple-making-disciples and a light in a world tainted by sin so that the lost will be brought to a saving knowledge of Jesus Christ.

ACTION

To those who will argue that any deliberate action to help integrate the church will result in something other than a "natural" change, and thus a "forced" action will inevitably fail, I simply say that what we have been doing for the past 100 + years, waiting for a "natural" movement and assimilation, has clearly not worked. It is the epitome of doing something the same way, over and over again, expecting different results. That is simply insane and it is long overdue for the American Christian church to think outside the torpid box and try a different approach. How much longer should we wait?

Any lasting and meaningful change will take action and sacrifice on our part, but the status-quo is unacceptable. It has produced pathetically little improvement and reconciliation within the church. Action is deliberate and intentional and is the "works" part of our faith. "What does it profit, my brethren, if someone says he has faith but does not have works? Can faith save him? If a brother or sister is naked and destitute of daily food, and one of you says to them, 'Depart in peace, be warmed and filled,' but you do not give them the things which are needed for the body, what does it profit? Thus also faith by itself, if it does not have works, is dead. . ... But do you want to know, O foolish man, that faith without works is dead?" (James

2:14-17,20). Yes, my friend, your own foolishness has deceived you if you prefer to live out your faith in inactivity!

There is a difference between "symbolic tolerance" where an accepting attitude towards ethnic topics involves no actual interaction or participation, and "functional acceptance," which involves action and a hands-on approach to propagate change. One is inaction, the other action. Ethnic integration in the church has been painfully slow since the 1944 founding of the Church for the Fellowship of All People in San Francisco (the nation's first intentionally multiethnic congregation). The good news is that the ideology within the church is slowly beginning to change. There are churches in America who have worked hard at creating a multi-ethnic body where all believers feel comfortable and included; an affirming environment where they understand that maintaining cultural identity for those who appear unlike themselves benefits the entire body and glorifies Christ. Kudos to those of you who have labored long and hard to bring about Christ-honoring unity to the church through deliberate inclusion.

There are churches that have refused to accept the norm when it comes to the segregation of the American evangelical church. These churches have deliberately sought to integrate their congregation with people representative of their neighborhood, giving new meaning to the term "blended" worship service. People like Mark DeYmaz, founding pastor and directional leader of the Mosaic Church of Central Arkansas - a multi-ethnic and economically diverse church, are making a major difference in the world where God has placed them in.[15] There's another church that my wife and I visit whenever we're in the Baltimore area. I have referred to this church and its pastors several times throughout this book. It's called Faith Christian Fellowship (FCF). The first time we visited FCF our hearts rejoiced from what we witnessed. Some of the experiences in the worship service were refreshingly unique to what we were used to and the overwhelming unity between Hispanics, Asians, African Americans, Near-Easterners and Caucasians was something to celebrate.

Along with my daily Scripture I also read a devotional from someone like Henri Nouwen, Oswald Chambers, C.S. Lewis, or others. The other day I read a Daily Guideposts devotional by Dolphus Weary which touched upon deliberate action motivated by God's love which builds bridges. The story goes like this:

"Emily is white; the Johnsons are black. They got to know each other about twenty years ago when they attended the same church. As Emily's health began to fail, the Johnsons cared for her.

Emily now has Parkinson's disease and lives in an assisted-living facility. The Johnson's take her to church, to the doctor and wherever else she needs to go. My wife Rosie and I visited the Johnsons not long ago and observed how tenderly they care for Emily. We saw them gently put her in a wheelchair and take her shopping, patiently listening to her whispers as she told them what she wanted. We moved from one aisle to the next in the store as she slowly read the labels on the cans. The kindness the Johnsons display toward this woman is truly phenomenal. No one pays them to do it; no court or agency assigned the job to them. They were moved by God to walk beside a person in need." [16]

As I read this, I was reminded of 1 Peter 1:22: 'Love one another deeply, from the heart.' The Johnsons demonstrated a deep agape, reaching out and caring for someone, and here I was observing it from a historical barrier of race – no boss, no employee, only God's kind of love."[17] These are the memories we need to make a reality in our lives and the lives of others.

You may have heard of The Memphis Miracle, where representatives from Pentecostal churches in the Memphis area came together to form an interdenominational partnership to replace the former all-white organization. What should not be missed is that the leaders and their congregations asked for forgiveness from the black Pentecostal bodies before pursuing anything else. Forgiveness is a huge aspect of reconciliation. Have you ever noticed that when you have sinned against someone and have not reconciled with them by asking them for forgiveness it is extremely difficult to look that person in the eye when you come in contact with them? Do you have difficulty looking a person of color in the eye when you speak to them? Pay closer attention to your interaction the next time you have such an encounter, whether it be at work, at the grocery store, or at your child's game. Forgiveness is an act of liberation, not just for the forgiven, but also for the one offering the forgiveness. Simply put, the task of ethnic reconciliation within the church is one which calls for forgiveness, turning from our sin, and lovingly accepting others through the empowerment of the Holy Spirit. Love will mean a willingness to forgive offences which may have been committed against us by members of other ethnic groups. We must remember that this is one of the obligations laid upon all who seek God's mercy (Matt. 6:12) and if we do not want to be liable for our debts, we must forgive others (Matthew 6: 14-15).

Change is often slow and painful, and is frequently accompanied by frustration, lack of support, and unseen obstacles, but if we are constantly working towards this unity, God will bless our efforts. Inactivity will always produce failure. Interethnic congregations will not and cannot happen without action! Nothing will change by simply talking about reconciliation. Rev. Stan Long (FCF) states that "Leadership has to catch a vision for it. . .it's not that easy. . .it takes a lot of sacrifice. The growth curve does not happen quickly." Rev. Long warns that the denomination needs to understand and be aware of this slow process as expecting immediate results are simply not realistic. If your motive is simply to have your church grow in numbers then the homogenous concept is still the fastest way to success in numbers, but if you want to grow in multicultural diversity, it will take time, energy, and patience, to see substantial change, as it did for Faith Christian Fellowship. But the Christ-honoring results are more than worth it. If your denomination refuses to adopt change which deliberately welcomes all ethnic groups, then perhaps your church needs to leave the sect and begin a nondenominational church. Certainly these are drastic measures but that is what it's going to take to bring about authentic reconciling change in the American Evangelical Church! These reconciling actions *are* happening across our country, just not as extensive as they need to be. Are they happening in your church and in your city or town? If not, demand it!

Take an initial step of faith and do something that will stimulate change. Visit an all-African American church (or an all-white church if you are black). You may be very surprised at how much a positive experience this will be. Yes, there are worship differences, but if we are truly putting others before ourselves, we'll put aside our preferences and embrace unity. This relatively simply step will begin the journey of healing which will have profoundly beautiful results. Get out of your comfort zone and courageously trust that the Holy Spirit will guide your path. Put that faith into practice.

Stepping out in faith by taking small steps toward deliberate interaction is a wonderful place to start. Build a relationship with one other person of a different ethnicity (but of the same sex you are). Pray for guidance as you search for that person that you frequently come in contact with at work, in the neighborhood, at the gym, or at your child's sports games. Invite them to lunch or for a cup of coffee, perhaps first meeting on neutral turf. If you have similar interests invite them to a ballgame. . .a "safe" location for you both. But understand that an intimate relationship which transcends superficial norms will only be realized if you allow that person entry into your protected world. Lower the drawbridge and invite them to cross the moat which you have so painstakingly built over the expanse of your life and allow them to enter your personal castle. In other words, invite them into your home. Be bold! Be courageous! Begin somewhere. Have a barbecue. Break bread. Break the ice.

NOTES:

CHAPTER 6: PICTURE THE POSSIBILITIES

[1]   Ralph P. Martin, *Philippians* (Grand Rapids, MI.: William B. Eerdmans Publishing, 2002), 163.

[2]   Richard J. Mouw, "This World Is Not My Home," *Christianity Today*, 24 April 2000,.

[3]   Also see the Book of Galatians.

[4]   Milne, *Knowing the Truth*, 333.

[5]   D. Williams, *Starting (& ending) a Small Group* (Downers Grove: InterVarsity, 1996).

[6]   John Perkins and Thomas A. Tarrants III, with David Wimbush, *He's My Brother: Former Racial Foes Offer Strategy for Reconciliation* (Grand Rapids: Baker, 1994).

[7]   Michael J. Wilkins, *The NIV Application Commentary: Matthew* (Grand Rapids: Zondervan, 2004), 637-638.

[8]   Bahá'í Faith, "Principle of the Bahá'í Faith" doc. on-line]; available from http://www.bahai.com/Bahaullah/principles.htm; accessed 18 Jan 2013.

[9]   Glen V. Wiberg, "Sightings in Christian Music," *Pietisten* 17:1 Summer 2002 [journal on-line]; available from http://www.pietisten.org/summer02/sightings.html; accessed 22 February 2013.

[10]   Abraham H. Maslow, *Motivation and Personality* (New York: Harper and Row Publishers, 1970).

[11]   Breckenridge, *What Color is Your God?*, 72-73.

[12]   Ibid., 73.

[13]   Frances E. Kendall, *Diversity in the Classroom* (New York: Teachers College Press, 1983), 20.

[14]   Craig Blomberg, *Matthew. The New American Commentary* (Nashville: Broadman & Holman Publishers, 1992).

[15]   See www.mosaicchurch.net, www.mosaix.info, and Mark DeYmaz's weekly blog, "Glue," at www.markdeymaz.com.

[16]   Dolphus Weary, "Fri 4," *Daily Guideposts 2011* (Guideposts: New York, NY, 2010), 347.

7

FINAL THOUGHTS

"For this very reason, make every effort to add to your faith good-
ness; and to goodness, knowledge; and to knowledge, self-control;
and to self-control, perseverance; and to perseverance, godliness;
and to godliness, mutual affection; and to mutual affection, love.
For if you possess these qualities in increasing measure, they will
keep you from being ineffective and unproductive in your knowl-
edge of our Lord Jesus Christ. But whoever does not have them
is nearsighted and blind, forgetting that they have been cleansed
from their past sins."
2 Peter 1: 5-9

A man died and went to heaven. He was in complete and total awe at the all-encompassing beauty of his new home and with the lovely, melodic sounds from the multitudes, singing praises to their Lord and King. But it was God's appearance that surprised him the most. "You don't look anything like what I expected you to look like," the man said. "What did you think I would look like?" God asked. "Well, older and. . ..white, I guess." "Why would you think that?" responded God. The man had no reply. "I see," said God. "Your perceptions while on earth were also often inaccurate. People's perception of things based on anything other than fact is foolish. My son, you failed at the most important commandment I gave you, to love others." "But I loved you," the man pleaded. "Don't you understand," responded God, "that my command to love me and to love people is inseparable? You can't love me unless you love others. You were to express love in the same way you received my love. . .at no cost to the recipient. You saw people conditionally. People had to pass your moral criteria before you would love them. They had to find a job first. They had to have graduated from high school. If you gave them a pass for the way they looked, which was rare, they had to act like you in order to be welcomed into your inner circle. Those who had abortions did not qualify. Those who struggled with addictions were ruled out. Let me ask you, who is worthy of *my* love? I created people with diverse physical charac-teristics as a blessing to humankind, but instead, humans made it a curse. My love extends to all my creation. I want no one to perish.

This blessing, too, has often been rejected. Why did you reject your brother and sister?" The man was silent.

"Your sin was having not attempted to reconcile with your fellow man and to work towards unity in the world I gave you, for if you had tried, *you would have succeeded.*" The man didn't need clarification. He knew what God was referring to because, as if in a second, he saw what seemed to be a video of the many times he rejected people. . .people of color. . .people who were different than himself. The man was speechless. God placed the man on his knee and talked lovingly about the passion he and his son had for all people. He explained how there is only one race, the human race, and how sin had caused the death of reconciliation and relation-ships. He explained how it wasn't supposed to be that way. . .how sin ruined everything, but that now. . .now things would be made new once again. The man wept.

After what seemed like a very long time, God wiped away the man's tears, dried his eyes, and ushered him into a long hallway where many beautiful jewels, crowns, and rewards were carefully placed on golden shelves. The man understood, instantaneously, that although all of these rewards were breathtakingly beautiful, some were greater than others. They were positioned from greatest to least. God took the man by the hand and began walking past the closest treasures, which were the largest, toward the ones which were clearly smaller. He walked and walked. The man's eyes admired the beauty and craftsmanship in all the rewards but was becoming concerned that God had not yet stopped at his. After what seemed like several days journey, God stopped and selected a small brooch from off the shelf. God pinned it on the man's chest, kissed him and said, "Welcome home, my son."

Ever since the fall, humans have been bent towards disunity, not unity; chaos not harmony; war not peace. Within the church we often appear more committed toward division over conjecture than we are over biblical truths. Somehow and at some point in our history, we lost the unity that is fundamental for the church and left no room for disagreement. We hunger for a utopia, a heaven on earth where love, peace and harmony exist. But that which we yearn for the most, we actually work towards its destruction. The only point of relevance here is that the American Evangelical church has often drawn its line in the sand over concerns that are strictly preference or interpretation, things which are not crucial to the faith. We allow no room for movement or compromise because, of course, we have a monopoly on truth. We need room for discussion and acceptance of those who do not view everything from the same lenses we do. I'm not speaking of those foundational biblical truths which concern salvation and such, but things which lie in a much more "gray" area. These arrogant and staunch stands do nothing but divide us. It also makes it incredibly difficult to accept others who are different than us, either physically or socially. I can't help but imagine what could be.

Howard Thurman reflects upon man's vision for a more harmonious life. "Ever since men began to reflect upon the meaning of their own lives and experiences and to set them down in written form, the dream of what life could be *if* has occupied a significant place in their calculations. Community as it is experienced in the far-flung hopes of men in all ages finds its greatest fulfillment in a picture of what the collective life of man would be like if it functioned in keeping with man's high destiny. Man 'has continued to dream ever of a better world, to speculate as to its possible nature, and to communicate his longings to other men in the hope that the ideal might, at least in part, become reality.'"[1] There lies the premise of this book. My dream is not unlike others before me. We all search for a forum to communicate our longings to those who will listen. I refuse to believe that the American Evangelical church cannot reverse our 300 year orbit of dizzying segregated worship and radically embrace our ethnically diverse brothers and sisters. This is not an unreasonable dream!

Recently I visited a mainline denominational church in the Philadelphia area. It is a well-respected, Bible preaching, God-praising church, save for one thing: everyone had the same skin tone and round eyes. As I walked a block and a half down the street I found an African-American youth playing hoops in the street with a bent rim secured with nails on a telephone pole. The corner store brags of the best cheesesteaks in Philly and as I enter, I see that not much has changed since the store opened nearly a half-century ago. The proprietor was an older Italian man, probably in his late 60s. As I stand in front of the cooler, my hand rests upon the sliding glass door, trying to decide if I want a Coke or a Dr. Pepper, a half a dozen black kids come in and out buying everything from Mountain Dew to Tastykakes. I realize that this store rests at the border between a white neighborhood and a black one. The (white) church is less than a 5 minute walk from the store. A few blocks down from the store is an African American Evangelical church in what was once a shoe store. The neon cross above the door had a hole in it where someone had thrown a rock. I tell you this because I cannot get these images out of my mind. One church clearly has financial resources, the other doesn't. Like most churches, the women outnumber the men at this one, only by a greater percentage. One has challenges with crime and struggles with being relevant within its community and the other has valet parking and mass media ministries. The two churches are so close in proximity to each other, yet so far in every other way. Why aren't the challenges the same in both churches? Why don't the two churches combine their congregations, resources, and gifts and have a greater impact for Christ, both within and outside their protective walls? Can you imagine a church that has co-pastors, one white and one black? There are churches like that in America; unfortunately they are few and far between.

We are betraying Jesus through our segregated worship services. The Apostle Paul spoke of "pressing on toward the mark for the prize of the high calling of God in Christ Jesus," (Philippians 3:14 PAR), yet the American Evangelical church has missed the mark. We have missed it because of our refusal to be dedicated, disciplined, and obedient to biblical teaching. The good news is that the race is not yet finished. Our mission, our purpose, our passion, our goal in life should be to love God and to love others, for that is the meaning of life.

The evangelical church is now at a crucial crossroad which its impact on America's future will be decided. The apathetic expression of the typical American Christian's faith will soon make the church so impotent that she will be nothing more than an afterthought *unless* drastic rectification soon takes place. The diluted theology preached from many pulpits, the desire to assimilate into our secular pagan culture, and lethargic spiritual disciplines has resulted in a "saltless" Christian, and we all know what happens when salt loses its saltiness (see Matthew 5:13). Perhaps what we have called God's blessings, wealth and freedom, has actually turned out to be a curse. Perhaps what the American Evangelical church really needs is persecution and poverty.

The browning of America is a reality which provides excellent opportunities for the American church. As communities change with ethnic diversity, the church can change along with it creating worship styles and programs that engender an atmosphere of inclusivity and love for all people. The income gap between the haves and have-nots is rapidly expanding in our country and with it, significant domestic mission needs. The local church will need discerning leadership to decide where best their precious mission dollars should be spent: locally or globally. Perhaps, at a time when missionaries from all over the world are being sent *to the* United States, there is a growing need for our homegrown missionaries to minister next door. Does it make sense to spend limited financial resources to send missionaries thousands of miles away when poverty, despair, and a lost world is within walking distance from many of our churches? In chapter 5 we spoke about Paul's assertion that those who don't take care of their own family are worse than a non-believer (1 Timothy 5:8). Similarly, those Christians who neglect the family of God, our "spiritually extended family," are people not acting like they understand the blessings and responsibilities that come from being adopted children of God. White reminds us that "One of the most subtle temptations of the Devil is his suggestion that we can best comply with the demands of duty in some place far away from our home."[2]

We must think locally before we can think globally. Our job is to live a life that is evangelical by nature. . .to live a life which causes the world to irresistibly ask us for the reason why we have such hope (1 Peter 3:15). We are called to be witnesses of Jesus Christ to a lost world and if we are not doing that in our lifestyles and life action, we are missing the life God calls us to and created us to live! If you want to make a difference for the kingdom, do not ignore or neglect that "world" which God has placed you in. Begin your evangelism with a small geographical circle, around your house, around your neighborhood and slowly expand that circle. We can, we must change the way the American Evangelical church has revealed herself to our communities.

The growing acceptance of what have long been social taboos is imploring the church to become relevant in America, yet we will never accomplish this through condemning others. Of course we need to be true to the Word of God, uncompromising with truths it orates. That should go hand-in-hand with being faithful to ethnic reconciliation and community development within the Gospel framework. Now is the time to put pride, preferences, and fear aside for the benefit of the kingdom. We must love. . .period. Love the homosexual, love the divorcee, love the convict, and love your Christian brother and sister. . ..LOVE. It is not a request by God. It is not an option or a choice. It is a commandment which we have collectively done a pathetic job of obeying. I wonder whether those Christians who have served honorably in the church for decades but have failed at loving their neighbor, regardless of color (that which Christ himself identified as equal to the greatest commandment), will be hearing the sweet and treasured words "Well done, good and faithful servant."

Let us rise up as a kingdom of Priests, that which we are called to be. "You also, like living stones, are being built into a spiritual house to be a holy priesthood, offering spiritual sacrifices acceptable to God through Jesus Christ. . .But you are a chosen people, a royal priesthood, a holy nation, a people belonging to God, that you may declare the praises of him who called you out of darkness into his wonderful light (1 Peter 2: 5, 9).[3] The phrase "royal priesthood" is reminiscent of God's conversation with Moses in Exodus 19: 5-6a, where the connotation is that God has singled out his chosen people to be heirs of a kingdom and home he has prepared for us. Douglas Stuart shares, "First, although God is Creator and Father of all people and people groups, he announced here his intention to create for himself, a particular people, a 'treasured possession.' This represents the separation of his chosen people from the general world population, or, stated in terms of the overall biblical plan of redemption, the beginning of the outworking of his intention to bring close to himself a people who will join him for all eternity as adopted members of his family."[4]

This idea of you and I being priests is expressed here by saying that Christ had made us exactly that, and so as fellow heirs to a heavenly kingdom we are to be invested with the ranking implied in these words. "Peter saw these promises as fulfilled in Jesus Christ, and God's elect nation is no longer coterminous with Israel but embraces the church of Jesus Christ which is composed of both Jews and Gentiles."[5] Just like any other priest, we are to be engaged in the holy service of God and are to offer him an acceptable worship, which can be seen as evangelistic in nature; that by our unity and praising of God's name, the world will want to join us in worshiping him. Thomas Schreiner astutely points out that "Western believers tend to individualize the notion of priesthood rather than seeing the community emphasis. . . Protestants are prone to individualize the text in a way that blunts or even denies its corporate emphasis."[6]

God's covenant people should not be distinguished by ethnic or territorial characteristics, or national affiliations, but exclusively by their faith in Christ. I refuse to compromise and settle for simply a dream of what can be. . . a hope that one day, long after I am dead and gone, that our children will experience a reality where interethnic congregations in America's Evangelical churches are the norm. I want it now! I demand it now, and so should you! This is not an implausible possibility! I will never accept the status quo and neither should you. Let's stop sloughing it off for the next generation to figure out and fix. Let our generation be the one to say this segregation stops here. Let us raise our voices so that it echoes down every church hall that *we are the ones* empowered to bring healing, love and reconciliation to our nation through our churches! Let us gather together, unified in Christ Jesus, with single purpose, and consolidate our power and resource for harmonious change, for our time is short. "The end of all things is near. Therefore be alert and of sober mind so that you may pray. Above all, love each other deeply, because love covers over a multitude of sins. Offer hospitality to one another without grumbling" (1 Peter 4: 7-9). Let people in our community say of us, "See how they love one another!" (John 13: 35).

Let us change the tide of disunity and indifference. Let us gather at the cross, that place where we shed our cloaks of superiority and pride and arrive at the common denominator of all humanity; where we share our neediness and brokenness. Let us bend our collective knees as desperate people alongside all our adopted brothers and sisters. Let a revival sweep across this great land and let this revival begin today with you and me! Let us gather from every corner of this nation, let us shout from the summit of Denali to the lowlands of Death Valley; from the Atlantic to the Pacific, that our Lord and Savior, Jesus Christ, has transformed us from worldly beings, lost in our self-centeredness, to *fellow heirs* joined together by Christ's blood and focused on a common goal, to glorify God the Father in all of our actions and by our unity! Let us be dedicated to exemplify the second greatest commandment, to love one another, as we pursue the greatest command, to love God with all that is in us. Our love for Christ consumes us and compels us to respond in such a way.

NATIONAL CHRISTIAN DAY OF RECONCILIATION

I have a dream where all American churches would express multiculturalism in their congregations. . .that rather than one national culture, several diverse cultures can morph into one worshiping body of Christ while maintaining the uniqueness of their God-given ethnic heritage. A cooperative *reversal* of what we have chosen *not to do* about ethnic reconciliation, could have profound impact, including the spiritual revival that our nation so desperately needs. I am calling for a **National Christian Day of Reconciliation**; a day of deliberate church integration. I am humbly requesting *your* assistance to make this a reality. This proposal is not very difficult at all. Churches that have a dominantly same-ethnic congregation would partner with another church of dissimilar ethnicity to swap one half of your congregation on the first Sunday of October, every year. Let's call it "**Reconciliation Sunday**" for short. This relatively simple step may very well begin the journey of healing which can then have profoundly beautiful results. Let this idea spread across our land! Let us celebrate diversity and the creativity of our Heavenly Father that is manifested in his greatest creation, US! Let us show the world how people who have differences can be united and can love without reservation because of Christ's love for us. Let us show the world that our faith is dynamic, relevant and effectual. Won't you join me, my friend?

For more on National Christian Day of Reconciliation go to www. reconciliationsunday.com.

NOTES:

CHAPTER 7: FINAL THOUGHTS

---

[1] Thurman, The Search for Common Ground, 43.

[2] White, Epistles to Timothy, 129.

[3] See also Revelation 1:6.

[4] Stuart, D. K., *Exodus. The New American Commentary* (Nashville: Broadman & Holman Publishers, 2006).

[5] T. R. Schreiner, *1, 2 Peter, Jude. The New American Commentary* (Nashville: Broadman & Holman Publishers, 2003).

[6] Ibid.